People's Livelihood in Contemporary China

Changes, Challenges and Prospects

Series on Chinese Economics Research

(ISSN: 2251-1644)

Series Editors: Yang Mu *(Lee Kuan Yew School of Public Policies, NUS)*
Fan Gang *(Peking University, China)*

Published:

Series on Chinese Economics Research – Vol. 6

People's Livelihood in Contemporary China

Changes, Challenges and Prospects

Editor

Li Peilin

Chinese Academy of Social Sciences, China

社会科学文献出版社
SOCIAL SCIENCES ACADEMIC PRESS (CHINA)

World Scientific

Published by

World Scientific Publishing Co. Pte. Ltd.
5 Toh Tuck Link, Singapore 596224
USA office: 27 Warren Street, Suite 401-402, Hackensack, NJ 07601
UK office: 57 Shelton Street, Covent Garden, London WC2H 9HE

Library of Congress Cataloging-in-Publication Data
People's livelihood in contemporary China : changes, challenges and prospects / editor, Li Peilin,
Chinese Academy of Social Sciences, China.
    pages cm -- (Series on Chinese economics research, ISSN 2251-1644 ; v. 6)
    Includes bibliographical references and index.
    ISBN 978-9814522250 (alk. paper)
    1. China--Social conditions--2000– 2. Consumption (Economics)--China. 3. Income
distribution--China. 4. Economic development--China. I. Li, Peilin, 1955– editor of compilation.
    HN733.5.P46 2014
    306.0951--dc23
                                                                        2013042871

British Library Cataloguing-in-Publication Data
A catalogue record for this book is available from the British Library.

当代中国民生
Originally published in Chinese by Social Sciences Academic Press (China).
Copyright © 2011 Social Sciences Academic Press (China).

China Book International provided funding for the translation of this book.

In-house Editor: DONG Lixi

Typeset by Stallion Press
Email: enquiries@stallionpress.com

Printed in Singapore by World Scientific Printers.

Contents

Series on Chinese Economics Research Editorial Committee

List of Tables

List of Figures

Introduction: The Changing Chinese Society

Li Peilin

The year 2009 marked the 60th anniversary of the establishment of the People's Republic of China. According to the Chinese Lunar Calendar, 60 years marks the beginning of a new cycle, or *Samsara*. Since being established in 1949 — and especially since the reform and opening up 30 years ago — China has experienced the most drastic changes ever in its 5,000-year history. During this time, China has transformed from an agricultural society into an emerging, dynamic, and industrialized nation and has undergone rapid urbanization. Chinese people's standard of living continues to rise and is taking rapid strides forward to a higher level of comprehensive well-being. The population structure has had a historic transformation with a low birth rate, low mortality rate, and low growth rate. The average life expectancy has reached the level of many developed countries, and China has changed from a poor and overpopulated nation to great nation rich in human resources. Hundreds of millions of Chinese people have been freed from poverty, which has made a significant contribution to lowering global poverty levels. The social security system covering urban and rural residents is taking shape, which will greatly improve the situation of Chinese farmers — a still large proportion of the Chinese population.

China's development over the past 60 years has indicated that the livelihood of the people is the key point of economic and social construction;

development must always give priority to the livelihood of the people. Having enough food and clothing is the first step in improving the livelihood of the people. Only after basic needs are met can a higher level of well-being be achieved. This "higher level of well-being" consists of employment as the foundation, education as the main point, income distribution as the source, social security as the support, and public safety as the assurance.

I. Social Construction: Theory and Practices

At the beginning of the establishment of modern China, people's livelihood was in shambles after the chaos caused by numerous wars. Under the leadership of the newly empowered Communist Party of China, China recovered rapidly through developing production and manufacturing, stabilizing prices, and improving the standard of living of the people. Along with the stable growth of the economy, social projects were also developed. Before the reform and opening up, the standard of living was improved with steady and incremental steps and full employment was realized. The social security system, compulsory education, and medical care system were established and allowed for greater industrialization. While social construction made great progress, China was also experiencing hard times. The Cultural Revolution led to food and clothing shortages, and poverty was still a fundamental problem in China. After the reform and opening up in 1978, the key emphasis in social projects had been transferred from "the class struggle" to economic development, and along with swift economic growth, social construction experienced unprecedented rapid development.

In China's academic language of sociology, "social construction" is not a new concept. In the 1930s and 1940s, "social construction" was an important issue. At that time, no other person was as important as the sociologist Sun Benwen (孙本文) in initiating social construction. In 1933, he organized and served as chief editor for the magazine *Social Construction*. He familiarized China with the concept of "social construction" and extended the historical connotation of the word. In the past, while "socialist construction", "modernization construction", "national reconstruction", and "economic development" were common phrases heard in progressive circles, "social construction" was rarely mentioned. When discussing the mission of socialist construction, people frequently mentioned objectives in the economic, political, and cultural domains, but usually did not regard "the society" as an independent domain to deploy their mission. Now, China's conception of "social construction" is extended to the strategic concept of constructing a harmonious socialist society. It is now observed that "social construction" — according to logical development paths and operational mechanisms of society — is to impel development and push progress in developing social projects, consummating social governance, improving social management, and maintaining social order.

As for the concept of "society", its scale and scope in different contexts is very diverse; it can refer to national and macrolevel society or local societies. Studies on society have different analytical and theoretical frames. First is the dualistic analysis frame of state and society. Examples of this frame include "the primacy of society over the state", according to John Locke; "the civil society balancing the state", according to Montesquieu and Tocqueville; and "the state's superiority over civil society", in Hegel's philosophical tradition. Marx inverted Hegel's frame and proposed that the foundation (civil society) determines the state's superstructure (state apparatus and ideology), and he developed this into the theory that claims "the economic base determines the superstructure". In the modern era, Jürgen Habermas further extended the theory of "civil society" to the concept of "the public sphere" (Offentlichkeit).

Another theoretical framework is the ternary analytical frame of "politics, economy, and society". For example, general modernization theory usually holds that democracy, market economy, and civil society are the modern foundations of a complete society. This analytical frame was further developed in the application of the social governance of public choice theory. Elinor Ostrom, a recent winner of the Sveriges Riksbank Prize in Economic Sciences and a founder of public choice theory claimed that, to analyze public affairs, the traditional theoretical model has three foundational works, namely Garrett Hardin's *The Tragedy of the Commons* (1968), *The Prisoners Dilemma* by Dawes *et al.* (1973, 1975), and Mancur Olson's *Logic of Collective Action* (1965). Ostrom proposed that a more effective framework considers the management of public welfare through social self-governance, and that acting in accordance to local conditions is decided mainly by the effects, benefits, and fairness of social management.

Other analytical frameworks are based on "Chinese experiences", namely, the comprehensive advancement of economic development, political construction, cultural reconstruction, and social construction. These frameworks regard economic development as the foundation and currently give priority to harmonious social construction. This is both the working layout and a framework of theoretical analysis. Cultural construction provides a broad space for research and understanding the "soft strength" of China.

China's understanding of social construction has been gradually refined. After modern China was established, China's socialist construction was carried on mainly through political and economic actions; social construction was not regarded as an independent domain of development. As economic development progressed, the development of a harmonious society assumed increasing importance. Reports from the 12th National Congress of the Communist Party of China in 1982 emphasized the improvement of the standard of living of the people. In December 1982, the Fifth Session of the Fifth National People's Congress decided to change the name of the development plan from the "Five-Year Plan on National Economy" to the "Five-Year Plan on National Economy and Social Development". From the Sixth Five-Year Plan to the Eleventh Five-Year Plan, social development has gradually been enriched; population, employment, social security, income distribution, healthcare, science and technology, education, environmental protection, social management, and spiritual civilization have become the primary areas of social development and have thereby been extended to the overall development of China.

After entering the 21st century, China has set the goal of constructing a developed and affluent society and has sought to achieve the goal of a "more developed economy, more effective democracy, more progressive scientific and technological culture, better educational system, more prosperous economy, more harmonious society, and higher standard of living for the people" by 2020. The Third Plenary Session of the 16th National Congress of the Communist Party of China in 2003 established the concept of "people-oriented, comprehensive, harmonious, and sustainable development"; the Fourth Plenary Session of the 16th National Congress of the Chinese Communist Party in 2004 stressed the strengthening of social construction and established significant strategic concepts for constructing a harmonious socialist society. In 2006, the Sixth Plenary Session of the 16th National Congress of the Chinese Communist Party made decisions on major issues concerning the construction of a harmonious socialist society. In 2007, the 17th National Congress of the Chinese Communist Party in 2007 further pointed out how to quicken the social construction that stresses improvement in the livelihood of the people. The practice and exploration of socialist modernization with Chinese characteristics has clearly entered a new development phase.

At present, China has formed policies on social construction that fall into 10 policy categories:

1. Population policy
   China's population policy insists on stable and low birth rates, improving population quality, improving population structure, dealing with the aging population positively, as well as promoting reasonable population movement and Chinese people's integrated development.
2. Employment policy
   China's employment policy insists on positive employment methods of job creation; establishing a unified and open labor market of ordered competition and unified planning among urban and rural areas; consummating an effective employment service system; promoting many forms of employment; and effective overall planning of urban labor. These policies also include solutions for transfer employment of rural surplus labors, the re-employment of laid-off workers and the unemployed, and the employment of college graduates.
3. Labor relations policy
   China's labor relations policy includes protecting worker's rights and interests according to the law, establishing mechanisms so the government, trade unions, and enterprises can coordinate labor relations, protecting worker's legitimate interests according to the law, and forming harmonious socialist labor relations in which employees and employers can both benefit.

4. Income distribution policy

   China's income distribution policy insists on implementing a system that regards income distribution as a function of work and as the main determiner. It aims to ensure that many kinds of distribution modes coexist and also insists on all elements of production to participate in distribution according to the contributions made by labor. This policy aims to put forth efforts in raising the income level of the low income earners, gradually enlarging the proportion of medium income earners, effectively adjusting excessively high incomes, firmly banning illicit income, diligently reversing tendencies in which the income distribution differential expands, and promoting common enrichment.

5. Social security policy

   These policies regard social security, social rescue, and social welfare as the foundation. These policies include development of basic support for the elderly and basic medical service as key points. These policies are in collaboration with commercial insurance to quicken the establishment of a social security system covering both urban and rural residents.

6. Urban and rural administration policy

   Administration policy includes the overall planning of urban and rural development, implementing guidelines on industry and agriculture, as well as formulating policies in which the city supports the countryside through capital redistribution, thus eventually eradicating the dualistic structure and divide between urban and rural areas. These policies also aim to unify planning of urban and rural construction and advance reforms in registry, employment, social security, healthcare, and housing to ultimately reduce urban and rural differentials.

7. Education policy

   China's education policies insist on giving priority to the development of education, implementing comprehensive all-around development, strengthening the safeguard responsibilities of the government in compulsory education, popularizing and consolidating the nine-year compulsory education structure, developing vigorous vocational education, improving the quality of higher education, establishing higher levels of equality in terms of educational opportunity, and promoting a greater learning society.

8. Medical service and healthcare policy

   Healthcare polices insist on prioritizing public welfare in medical and healthcare services, deepening the systemic reforms of medical services and healthcare, strengthening government responsibility, rigorously enforcing supervision and management in the medical sector, constructing a basic healthcare system covering rural residents, and providing safe, effective, convenient, and moderately priced public healthcare and basic medical services.

9. Public safety policy

   Public safety policy focuses on establishing a public safety system that includes rigid social order, food and drug safety, production safety, traffic safety, as well as disaster prevention and reduction. It also gives priority to managing state affairs according to the law, advancing comprehensive rectification of public order, implementing criminal justice policy, cracking down on all kinds of criminal activities according to the law, advancing citizen participation in public order development, guaranteeing human rights in terms of life and property, and maintaining normal social order.

10. Environmental protection policy

    These policies insist on placing importance on the environment first and controlling unreasonable development. Other core focuses include strengthening prevention of pollution by addressing the sources; maintaining ecological protection and preservation; shifting from pollution management to pollution prevention; and constructing a resource-conserving and environmental friendly society.

These policies are all raised and formed based on the theoretical framework and practices of social construction, and China aims to realize these policies through unceasing adherence to practices of social construction.

II. Great Changes in People's Livelihood

A. *Obvious improvement of standard of living*

After the People's Republic of China was established in 1949, China began addressing the miserable circumstances of a war-torn nation. The people's

livelihood withered and the economy was badly stunted, requiring full-
scale national construction. In the early years of establishment, China's
national income per capita was equivalent to the level of developed countries in the mid-18th century. From 1949 to 1978, along with economic
development, China's standard of living also gradually increased. However,
this increase was slow, and in 1978, China's national income per capita was
still only US$190. After the reform and opening up, along with sustaining
quick economic growth, the standard of living also quickly increased; by
2008, China's per capita GDP amounted to more than US$3,000, which
placed it firmly in the rankings of a middle-income country.

In the 30 years after the reform and opening up, China's urban residential income rapidly increased. From 1978 to 2008, urban residents' per
capita disposable income increased from RMB 343 to RMB 15,781;
farmers' per capita net income increased from RMB 134 to RMB 4,761.
As a result, the per capita urban and rural residential building areas also
doubled to accommodate such growth. Family property increased overall,
and the standard of living improved quite obviously. The economic
shortages that puzzled China before the reform and opening up were being
fundamentally and systemically eradicated.

Consumption levels obviously increased according to income increase,
and the quality of life in China was further improved. Engel's coefficient

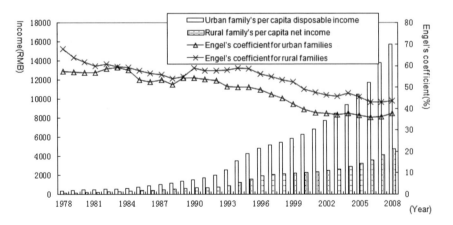

Figure 1. Urban and Rural Families' Per Capita Income and Engel's Coefficient From
1978 to 2008.

for rural families (the proportion of food expenditure in total consumer expenditures) dropped from 67.7% in 1978 to 43.7% in 2008, and Engel's coefficient for urban families dropped from 57.5% in 1978 to 37.3% in 2008. The proportion of rural families' per capita disposable income rose from 5.1% in 1980 to 9.5% in 2007, and this proportion for urban families also rose from 8.4% to 13.3%.

China's standard of living has reached an improved level as a whole and there is still great capacity for further improvement.

B. *Huge changes in the social structure*

For the past 60 years and especially since 1978, along with the advancement of industrialization and urbanization, the reform and opening up has provided a strong platform for development. China's social structure has undergone huge changes, and comprehensive national strength has obviously been strengthened. China has gradually transformed from an agricultural nation to an emerging industrial power, and the urbanization level has rapidly increased.

Since Modern China was established in 1949, China has undergone swift economic growth and tremendous changes in industrial structure. China's changes in industrial structure can be divided into two stages. The first stage was from the founding of Modern China until 1978; in this period, the proportion of primary, secondary, and tertiary industries in gross domestic product (GDP) changed from 53:18:29 in 1952 to 31:45:24 in 1978. At this stage, the change of industrial structure featured secondary industries' rapid expansion to become the foundation of the national economy. The status of agriculture dropped in the economy, but it still played a leading role, and the service industry had excessively slow growth relative to other industries. The second stage was from the reform and opening up to present day. In this period, the proportion of primary, secondary, and tertiary industries in GDP changed from 31:45:24 in 1978 to 11.3:48.6:40.1 in 2008 (see Figure 2). During this stage, the service industry experienced rapid growth; industry developed steadily, but the proportion of agriculture in the national economy dropped sharply. This reflected the optimization of China's industrial structure. This change of economic structure indicated that China's economy had entered a period of industrialization.

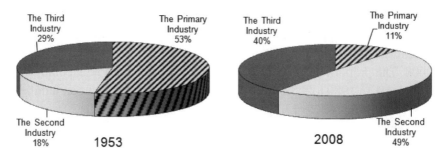

Figure 2. GDP Structural Changes.

In 1949, China had an urban population of 57 million and the urbanization level was 10.6% (see Figure 3), which was three points lower than the average global level in 1900; this figure represents China's status as an agricultural nation. From 1949 to 1978, the urbanization level increased gradually, eventually reaching 19.7% in 1978 (see Figure 3). Since the reform and opening up, urban and rural economies in China have both experienced rapid development, which has greatly promoted the urbanization process. From 1949 to 1978, urbanization grew by 7%. From 1978 to 2008, the urbanized level rose from 19.7% to 45.7%, which represented an increase of 26% since 1978. At present, China has 655 cities with population over 1 million people, 462 cities more than in 1978, when there were 157 cities with over 1 million people. Urban economic strength has unceasingly increased; at present, the cities at prefecture level and above account for 63% of the total GDP in China.

C. *Historical change of the population structure*

Over the past 60 years, China's population structure has experienced historical changes; it has changed from a nation with a high birth rate, high mortality rate, and low growth rate into nation with a low birth rate, low mortality rate, and high growth rate. From 1952 to 2008, the total population increased from 570 million to 1.328 billion, the birth rate dropped from 37% to 12.14%, the mortality rate dropped from 17% to 7.06%, and the natural growth rate dropped from 20% to 5.08% (see Figure 4). Economic development, social reform, and birth control policy are responsible for this historic change in population structure. China started

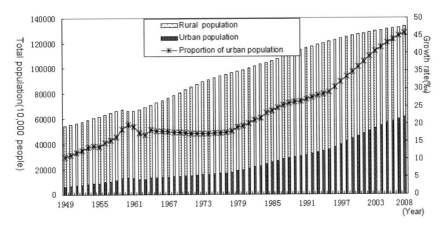

Figure 3. Urbanization Process From 1949 to 2008.

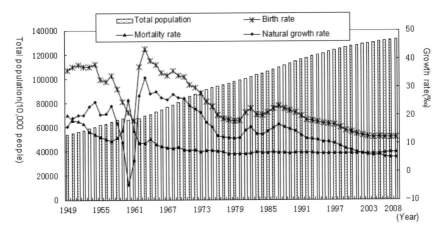

Figure 4. Changes in Population Structure From 1949 to 2008.

to implement birth control policy from the early 1970s and started to strictly implement a "one couple, one child" policy in urban registered population from the early 1980s. With the rapid decline in birth rate, China's population structure underwent huge changes, the total fertility rate fell from about 6 in the early 1970s to about 1.8 at present. China reduced the current population by roughly 300 million people with the "one child" policy, and the social dependency coefficient dropped continuously; this has made a great contribution to China's economic and social development. With the population under control, population quality has greatly increased. The proportion of college students, professionals, and skilled laborers are unceasingly increasing, and the average life expectancy has reached the same level as many developed countries.

In next few years, China will successively have three peaks of job-age population, total population, and old population. Experts project that, in 2016, the job-age population (15–64 years old) will reach about 1.01 billion — China's historical peak value. In the 2030s, total population will reach about 1.5 billion and reach a historical peak value. In the 2040s, the old population (65 years and older) will reach 320 million — the historical peak value. At present, China's population policy is to first invest in the integrated development of population, to stabilize low birth rate levels, to improve the overall quality of the population, to improve the population structure, to guide reasonable population distribution, to safeguard population security, to promote transformation into a nation of great human resources, and to promote harmonious and sustainable development of the population, as well as the economic and social resources environment.

D. *Remarkable achievements in antipoverty*

After the founding of Modern China, China has always devoted itself to the reduction of poverty; the impoverished population has accordingly assumed a declining trend. Since the reform and opening up, with economic growth and the implementation of antipoverty policy, several hundred million Chinese people were able to escape poverty, which has made significant contributions to lowering global poverty levels. From 1978 to 2007, the absolute quantity of the rural impoverished population which did not have enough food and clothing dropped from 250 million to 14.870 million; the proportion in total rural population dropped from 30.7% to 1.6%. The data released by the World Bank in 2007 indicated that in the past 20 years, 67% of global antipoverty achievements came from China. Furthermore, without China's contributions, the global impoverished population would still be increasing. China is also presently the only country to achieve the antipoverty goals set by the United Nations millennium development targets in advance.

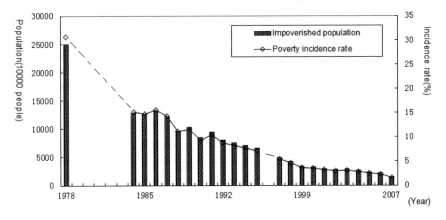

Figure 5. Antipoverty Situations of Rural Residents.

Since the 1980s, China has started to implement poverty relief and development strategies for economic growth. In 1984, the Central Committee and the State Council issued a "Notice on Helping Poor Areas to Improve" [《关于帮助贫困地区尽快改变面貌的通知》 (*guan yu bang zhu pin kun di qu jin kuai gai bian mian mao de tong zhi*)], and hundreds of poverty-stricken counties were screened out to implement key poverty relief plans. From 1985 to 1993, the rural impoverished population fell from 125 million to 80 million, and reduced on average by 6.4 million people per year. The poverty incidence rate dropped from 14.8% in 1985 to 8.22% in 1993. In the mid-1990s, the State Council decided that, from 1994 to 2000, the final 80 million rural residents would escape poverty. Therefore, the State Council formulated the "National Seven-Year Plan for Priority Poverty Alleviation" [《国家八七扶贫攻坚计划》 (*guo jia ba qi fu pin gong jian ji hua*)]. Through seven years of work in poverty reduction, the rural impoverished population was reduced from 80 million to 30 million, with a 3% poverty level in rural areas.

Although China's achievements in poverty alleviation were remarkable, policy regarding poverty alleviation has faced many challenges and difficulties. After entering the 21st century, China's rural poverty alleviation and development work entered a new stage; the central government formulated the "China Rural Poverty Alleviation and Development Program

(2001–2010)" [《中国农村扶贫开发纲要（2001–2010年）》(*zhong guo nong cun fu pin kai fa gang yao*)]; during the "Eleventh Five-Year Plan" (2006–2010), the completion of the village poverty alleviation plan was the target, which included 148,000 poor villages in 592 counties of priority poverty alleviation (covering about 80% of impoverished populations). This plan aimed to reduce the differentials between city and countryside, among rural areas, and among the low-income groups, while unceasingly reducing impoverished populations and thus realizing balanced growth.

E. *Formation of a social security system covering both urban and rural population*

After Modern China was established, China gradually established a complete social security system, which had provided the foundation of a safeguard for the development of industrialization and urbanization. The social security system formed under the planned economy, however, had small coverage, a low degree of usage and implementation, and weak safeguard functions.

After the reform and opening up, in lieu of some markedly unreasonable problems in the social security system, some preliminary reforms were carried out in 1984. The scope of social security was expanded, the standards were raised, insurance items were increased, the contradiction between the dependencies of different enterprises was alleviated, and some laws and regulations concerning social security were drafted to promote a normalized and just system. The social security system changed from an institutional arrangement, in which the country took charge and the work unit undertook the responsibilities, into an institutional arrangement, in which responsibility is shared under the socialist market economy.

In 1993, China officially established the socialist market economic system, determined the basic matters of the social security system, and set up a system of multilevel endowment insurance. China also established a medical insurance system which combined unified planning with individual accounts, as well as a social security management system which separated the functions of government from those of institutions and had unified management. Social security reform was carried out comprehensively, and the reform emphasized the realization of endowment insurance, medical insurance, and unemployment insurance. This was an era in which policy-makers explored and established the social security system to meet the demands of socialist market economic development. In 1994, the Fourteenth Plenary Session of the Third Central Committee of the Communist Party of China adopted the "Decision of the Central Committee of the Chinese Communist Party on Certain Issues Concerning Establishing the Socialist Market Economic System" [《中共中央关于建立社会主义市场经济体制若干问题的决定》 (*zhong gong zhong yang guan yu jian li she hui zhu yi shi chang jing ji ti zhi ruo gan wen ti de jue ding*)]. This decision proposed a systematic plan and framework for social security system reform and gradually changed the original system into a system comprising unified planning in combination with individual account management to adapt to the consequent economic system reforms.

The Sixth Plenary Session of the 16th Central Committee of the Communist Party of China in 2006 and the 17th National Congress of the Communist Party of China aimed at establishing a social security system that emphasized basic endowment insurance, basic medical insurance, and a minimum wage security system that covered both urban and rural residents. By the end of 2008, the number of people who participated in basic endowment insurance for urban residents, basic medical insurance for urban residents, unemployment insurance program, workers' compensation insurance, and maternity insurance was 218.9 million, 316.98 million, 124 million, 138.1 million, and 91.81 million, respectively. In the whole year, 23.34 million urban residents and 42.91 million rural residents were provided with minimum living security; nearly 50 million migrant laborers participated in the workers' compensation insurance, and more than 40 million migrant laborers participated in the urban medical insurance program. A total of 2,729 counties (city, district) carried out the practice of new rural cooperative medical services, in which about 814 million people participated, and the coverage rate was 91.5%. The accumulated outlay of the new rural cooperative medical fund was RMB 42.9 billion, in which a total of 370 million people profited from it. In 2009, 10% of China's counties (city, district) carried out pilot programs of the new rural social endowment insurance program. In this new program, insured farmers aged 60 years or older who fulfilled criteria in accordance with related conditions could receive a basic pension.

Establishing a social security system "covering urban and rural residents" was a significant decision made by the central government. Cancelling the agricultural tax ended a system that had lasted over 2,600 years in which farmers planted crops and paid taxes, establishing a social security system covering urban and rural residents ended thousands of years of tradition in which Chinese farmers lacked social security.

III. Challenges and Issues in Social Construction

China has entered a medial stage of industrialization and urbanization development. With rapid advancements in industrialization, urbanization, marketability, and internationalization, the economic system, social structure, benefit patterns, and ideological concepts are changing profoundly. This unprecedented social change inevitably brings about various contradictions and issues, while boosting China's development.

Urban and rural regional development has not been balanced. Although firm measures were taken to cancel the agricultural tax system and farmers have been given massive transfer payments in finance, the relative income of agricultural labor is still excessively low; therefore, measures to make farmers more financially stable have become a major issue in Chinese modernization development. Moreover, the development differential is also expanding between coastal and inland areas as well as between different provinces.

The income disparity gap is also widening. Irrespective of using the Gini coefficient or the multiple of income stratum, at present, income disparity in China is huge and worth attention. The growth of income disparity has become one important reason to implement many social policies.

Employment pressure is huge, and problems regarding labor relations are increasing. After the problems regarding food and clothing shortages were solved, employment became the biggest problem in Chinese people's livelihoods. At present, the supply of labor is increasing incessantly. Much of this pressure is caused by the transfer of agricultural labor to non-agricultural sectors. Meanwhile, with the change of labor relations under the market economy, the social conflict concerning labor relations increased. Establishing standard, ordered, fair, reasonable, mutually beneficial, harmonious, and stable new socialist labor relations have become an important subject of China's economic and social development.

The aging population trend of China is obvious and social security will have to face big challenges in the future. Often times, wealthy countries display aging trends; at present, China's wealth is several times lower than developed countries with similar degrees of aging. The aging population is challenging China's endowment insurance system. China's familial-based elderly support patterns and social ethics are also facing various new problems. On one hand, there is a need for China to diligently establish widespread coverage of social safety networks; on the other hand, it must prevent the swift growth of welfare to maintain economic growth. Handling the contradiction between the rigid growth of the social security system and the cyclic fluctuation of economic development is a challenge for China's development.

The contradiction between the environment, resources, and rapid development has become quite obvious. China has huge population scale and low per capita natural resource levels and faces the incisive contradiction among economic development, enhancement of standard of living, consumption capacity expansion, and the environment and resource supplies. It is impossible for such a huge population to replicate the lifestyle of high consumption that is seen in developed countries. Along with an increase in environmental consciousness, the huge toll that development has on the environment is beginning to be understood. Under the rigid restraints of environment and resource supplies, China must construct a society of resource conservation and of environmental friendliness to promote successful and sustainable development between human and nature.

IV. China Enters the New Growth Stage of Development

China's experiences over the course of more than 30 years of reform have indicated that soberly judging which development phase it is in is very important for determining realistic development targets and choosing the appropriate development strategy.

A. *Social reform and a new growth stage*

After the reform and opening up, a familiar concept to describe the new goals of development has been "reforming China"; this refers to the reform of the market orientation of the economic system and the expansion of the strength of market regulation in the operational mechanisms of economy. The current object of economic system's reform is to allow China to transform from a highly concentrated planned economy system into the socialist market economic system.

Deng Xiaoping (邓小平) designed "three steps" for a grand blueprint for China's modernization: step one, from 1981 to 1990, aimed to have the gross national product (GNP) doubled and all Chinese people to have enough food and clothing; step two, from 1991 to 2000, aimed for GNP to double and achieve a higher standard of living for all Chinese; step three, up to the middle period of the 21st century, aims to increase per capita GNP to the level of developed countries, with modernization basically achieved. Clearly, the main goals of this plan were to increase the national economy of China as well as the standard of living of the people.

This type of program is referred to as "social reform"; it mainly refers to the change of the social structure and is also the process of industrialization and urbanization. Namely, it refers to China's transition and reforming from an agricultural, rural, enclosed, and semi-enclosed society to an industrial, urban, and open society.

Currently, the socialist market economic system has been basically established; per capita GDP has amounted to more than US $3,000, which is equal to the level of low-middle-income countries, and China is striding toward the middle-income country. Industrialization and urbanization levels have entered a medial phase. At present, although China is still in the initial stages of socialism, the contradiction between the material and cultural demands and the relative laggard productivity level is still the principal barrier in economic and social development, but a series of new characteristics has appeared in the development process, and China has entered the new growth stage of development.

B. *Essential characteristics of the new growth stage*

Some characteristics have only started to appear at this new growth stage and these are not only different from prior to reform and opening up but also different from the initial period of reform and opening up.

The industrialization and urbanization process has entered an accelerated new growth stage. According to international precedents, the value-added agriculture in the GDP should drop below 5% of the total, the proportion of agricultural workers should drop below 30% of the total employment structure, and the urbanization level should surpass 50%, which symbolizes a significant reform of economic and social structure. From the angle of the output value structures, the employment structure, and the urban and rural structure, China has entered a stage of structural transformation. In terms of GDP, the proportion of value-added agriculture fell below 10% in 2010 and will drop to about 6% by 2015. In terms of the employment structure, the proportion of agricultural workers dropped below 38% in 2010 and is expected to drop to about 33% by 2015. In terms of the urban and rural structure, the urbanization level based on the urban resident population achieved reached 48% in 2010 and is expected to surpass 50% by 2013, reaching 53% in 2015. These figures indicate that China has entered a medium accelerated stage of the industrialization and urbanization and that the economic structure and social structure are undergoing profound transformation.

The social structure transformation has entered a new growth stage that aims to eradicate the urban and rural dualistic structure. The huge differential between urban and rural structures and urban and rural development is a long-term and prominent issue of China's non-balanced development. Along with the industrialization and urbanization entering a structural transformation stage, urban and rural integrative growth has become a new development demand. Eradicating the urban and rural dualistic structure is intended to not only eliminate the barrier between modern industry and traditional farming but also gradually eliminate the barriers between the city and countryside in terms of employment, education, medical services, social security, and household registry. Eradicating the urban and rural dualistic structure will become a major act that will have profound influence on Chinese history.

The standard of living in China has entered a new stage of growth and mass consumption. The GDP was RMB 30,067 billion in 2008, and total population was 1.328 billion, with a per capita GDP of RMB 22,640 or US $3,313. With a GDP growth rate of 8% in 2009, per capita GDP amounted to about US $3,500. In recent years, the growth of per capita GDP, especially if determined with U.S. dollars, has experienced rapid development. From 1980 to 2000, GDP increased from more than US$200 to more than US $800. In 2000, when formulating the goals of comprehensive construction of an affluent society up to 2020, policymakers forecasted that it would take 20 years to realize their goal of a quadrupled per capita GDP, namely per capita GDP would amount to more than US $3,000. But the actual per capita GDP surpassed US $1,000 in 2003, reached US $2,000 in 2006, surpassed US $3,000 in 2008, and approached US $4,000 in 2010.

Per capita GDP growth speed quickened first because of fast economic growth; second, because of the reduction of the population increase; and third, because of Renminbi revaluation. According to international conventions, when the per capita income surpasses US$3,000, the resident consumption will become normalized. In 2009, urban and rural residents' Engel's coefficient reduced to about 37% and 43%, respectively; according to the standards of the UN Food and Agriculture Organization, China achieved an upgraded consumer phase from well-off to affluent. The Chinese people have started to popularize large household consumption, including housing and automobiles, and the proportion of expenditures for education, medical services, communication, and travel and culture has increased rapidly, which indicated that China has started to enter a new growth stage of mass consumption as a whole.

China's education system has entered a new growth stage. The country has popularized nine-year compulsory education, and vocational and professional degree education have both rapidly expanded. In 2009, the gross enrollment rate of higher education reached 24%; this signified that higher education had entered a more mainstream stage. This helped overall national quality to improve by allowing the transformation from a large population agricultural nation to a great source of human resources.

Social security has entered new stage of development aimed at covering all Chinese people. In recent years, the work of expanding the coverage of social security has made effective progress; the minimum living security system covering city and rural populations has been established. Healthcare coverage has also improved; a medical security system covering all people based on corporate medical insurance for urban residents and the new rural cooperative medical system have been formed. The retirement security system covering urban and rural retirees has been implemented. Basic endowment insurance, basic medical insurance, and minimum living security has been set up for full implementation by 2020. These actions all signify that China has entered the new stage of social security system development.

China's reforms are now transitioning from economic reform to overall reform. Since the reform and opening up began 30 years ago, the economic system reform has remained the main focal point. Presently, the basic socialist market economy has been established, but huge changes in the economic and social structure are needed to adapt to this new system, and the reform has expanded from the economic sphere to overall reform. Currently, the prominent problem is carrying on social reform in employment, income distribution, social security, urban and rural social construction, social management, institution movement, community, and social organization.

V. Primary Mission of the New Stage of Growth

Investment, export, and consumption are usually considered the dominant factors that drive economic growth. In terms of exports, under the influence of the international financial crisis, China's exports underwent negative growth of more than 20% for more than 12 months in a row before starting to recover. It is anticipated that, as the policy of international trade protectionism gains ground generally, it is unlikely for China to restore the degree of dependence upon foreign trade that accounted for 60% of the economy prior to the crisis. Moreover, China is a large nation and quite different from other export-oriented East Asian and Southeast Asian nations; it is very risky for China to excessively rely on foreign trade. In times of crises, this economic model is difficult to sustain and very unstable. China exports for foreign exchange purposes and buys U.S. dollar national debts, but the U.S. prints more money to cause U.S. dollar depreciation, thus diluting the debt. According to some scholars, expanding domestic consumption will no doubt be beneficial, but the transformation needs time. It is very difficult to stimulate economic growth through domestic consumption in the short term; therefore, investment should be taken seriously but with patience. China has characteristically high savings ratios and high investment rates and has sustained abnormal economic growth for quite a long time.

We first discuss the hypothesis that "it is very difficult to stimulate economic growth with consumption in the short-term". This hypothesis makes sense at first but it is questionable after thorough consideration. First, this hypothesis was established based on past development experiences. When the economic growth rate was dismal in the past, China always used the means of finance and investment expansion to stimulate the economy. China has never realized the stimulation of economy by expanding consumption. When stimulating the economy through high investment, the result is always construction of redundant projects, capacity surplus, and increase in inventories; a drop in investment can cause inflation after crisis, and it is hard to say these unsolved problems will not stage a comeback after the international financial crisis is over.

We must observe a new possibility, a new future, namely, China's economic and social development entering a new growth stage. The defining characteristic of this stage is different from before, and the old methods that China used before also need to change.

Consumption levels were at one point restricted by income, but since times are changing, consumption could provide China with a strong economy. Based on online opinions and surveys, Chinese people seem optimistic about the domestic economy of China, meaning that there is a differential between statistical data and what they feel. What people feel is not completely unreasonable. In terms of gross national income, the proportion of resident income was dropping unceasingly; for instance, from 1992 to 2007, the proportion of resident's disposable income in GDP dropped from 69% to 53%; at the same time, the proportion of enterprise's disposable income in the national income rose from 12% to 23%, and the proportion of the government's disposable income as part of national income rose from 19% to 24%. Statistically, consumption is not booming because the country lacked the money. From 1994 to 2008, China's total tax revenue increased from more than RMB 500 billion to RMB 5.4 trillion, which grew on average by 18% every year, and was largely higher than the growth of GDP. As for common people, from 1994 to March 2009, the remaining sum of urban and rural personal savings increased from more than RMB 2 trillion Yuan to RMB 24.1 trillion, which also grew on average by 18% every year. From 1985 to 2008, resident's consumption rates, namely the proportion of resident consumption in GDP, unexpectedly dropped from 52% to 35.4%, which was a very low level internationally, much lower than the U.S.' 70% and Japan's 65%. In the U.S., 300 million people spent more than US$10 trillion in a year, and in China 1.3 billion people spent just over US$1 trillion in a year, illustrating the difference between the two consumer markets.

Depressed consumption originates from the income distribution structure. The biggest challenge in terms of consumption is the income distribution structure. For more than 30 years, swift economic growth has been China's greatest achievement, but the most challenging problem is income distribution. The Gini coefficient growth curve that weighs the income differential was almost as same as the GDP growth curve: both soared, and in the process of modernization, there has been no precedent of a country increasing its Gini coefficient from 0.2 to 0.5 in 30 years, as China did. According to the existing findings, about 60% of overall income differential may be explained by the income differential between the city and countryside, and this is the most problematic comparison point in the income differential. In recent years, the agricultural tax was cancelled, and investment and finance transfer payments to rural areas was increased. Under the influence of the international financial crisis, farmer's income from work in urban areas was largely influenced in 2009; thus, the farmer's overall income growth was influenced. The ratio between urban and rural residents' income and growth speed was expanded once more. Massive reduction in farming and transfer of rural labor to urban centers is important for increasing China's consumption capacity, and the improvement of farmer consumption capacity is the determining factor in boosting overall consumption capacity.

The consumption structure has something to do with the socially stratified structure. The arrival of mass consumption relies on the expansion of middle-income groups to a great extent, which is to say that the socially stratified structure should transform from a pyramid model to an olive model (with the middle class being the most massive part of the social structure). Theoretically, the arrival of a stage of mass consumption depends upon the growth of the middle class. Certainly "the middle class" is a very unclear concept; economists mainly define the middle class by income and assets, while sociologists pay more attention to their occupational targets. Only when tertiary industries of a country occupy the overwhelming majority of the entire industrial structure and the white-collar stratum occupies the majority in the total amount of people employed, can a country become a consumption-based economy. According to research, if the middle class is defined by income, occupation, and education, in 2006, China's middle class accounted for 12% of the total population, and about 25% of the urban population. Certainly, because China has a huge population, an increasing of a single percentage point can account for a huge jump in consumption.

The household consumption proportion successively decreases along with the increase of household income, and this rule is obvious in China. According to the 2008 sampling survey of Chinese society, the household consumption rate decreased successively along with the increase of income. The lower the family's income level, the higher is the consumption proportion, and the higher the family's income level, the lower is the consumption proportion. Moreover, there is a huge difference in consumption proportions. This signifies that allocation of income within the entire society is related to consumption. To expand consumption, the proportion of resident income in the national income must increase, and in terms of resident income, the proportion of low-income group's income must increase.

According to the analysis of cruising data, as for the average Chinese family, three main factors affect current consumption: expenditures for education, medical services, and housing. In education and medical services, in particular, the proportion of middle- and low-income families' expenditures is much higher than for high-income families. Conversely, families with higher incomes spend a larger proportion of income on housing. As for high-income households, investment in housing has transformed from the personal consumption into property income, but this mentality can swiftly lead to an asset bubble in housing; some feel that it is better to consider housing expenses as consumption, as well. Middle- and low-income families' high proportion of anticipated expenses for education and medical services have limited these families' current and immediate consumption; in a survey of goals in personal savings, expenditures for education and medical services are often placed as the top two goals. Common people's savings are intended to dodge the risk of household consumption in the future. This is indicative of China's spending culture, while countries such as the U.S. are thought to have a culture of credit consumption.

To change consumer behavior, a series of related systems should be established and consummated, and a series of social policies and social reforms are also necessary. The normal growth mechanisms of labor wages should be established; an annual growth mechanism of labor wages should be established according to the growth of enterprise profits. Simultaneously, financial wage growth mechanisms should be determined according to economic growth and the enterprise's expansion of labor wages. Otherwise, expanding the proportion of resident income in the national income and expanding the proportion of the worker income in enterprise income are erroneous. Furthermore, expanding consumption based on income increase is also empty talk. The structure of income distribution should be adjusted, and some levers, including finance, tax revenue, social security, and social welfare, should be used to adjust income distribution so that income can flow to low-income groups which need to boost consumption. Meanwhile, the middle-income group which supports mass consumption can be expanded. Consumer products and their collective services should be more effectively and widely provided, and the social security system covering urban and rural areas should be established and consummated to realize the equalization of urban and rural collective services in order to stabilize people's consumption by alleviating anticipated costs of future education, medical service, housing, and old-age support.

Expanding resident consumption is not only an economic issue but also a social and political issue. In terms of politics, as a socialist nation, China must achieve common prosperity, which is decided by the essence of socialism. In terms of social aspects, the excessive disparity in income has become an in-depth cause of some social problems and middle- and low-income people's universal disaffection. In terms of economy, the excessively big income differential has restrained consumption of middle- and low-income stratum and has had adverse effects on universal growth of consumption in that economic growth excessively relies on investment and exports. In 1993, Comrade Deng Xiaoping (邓小平) warned that "income distribution is important, we must prevent polarization, and in fact, polarization appears naturally. We must solve these problems with various means, methods, and programs". Otherwise "if it unceasingly develops like this, more problems will be brought one day".[1] In China's "Twelfth Five-Year Plan", income distribution will be principle problem addressed.

---

[1] See *Chronological Life of Deng Xiaoping: 1975–1997 (II)* [《邓小平年谱1975–1997 (下)》 (Deng Xiao Ping Nian Pu: 1975–1997 (II))], published by Central Documentation Press, 2004 version.

At this new growth stage of development, the following problems must be solved emphatically.

(1) Transforming the development path

Transforming the development path is not empty talk, but the practical and urgent demand of development at China's new growth stage. The so-called transformation of the development path must transform the economic growth excessively relying on investment and export to more reliance on the domestic consumption. This international financial crisis illustrated that it is not sustainable to excessively rely on investment and export, and the economic growth in next 30 years must be based on the domestic consumption. China must transform from low-cost quantity expansion of economic growth to quality improvement including the increase of technical content, and from "Made in China" to "Chinese branding". This path promotes industrial upgrading. China must also transform from a development path based on the price of resources and environment to a basis in resource conservation and environmental protection; focusing less on heavy industry and more on modern services to develop low-carbon economies.

(2) Raising the standard of living unceasingly

Since the reform and opening up more than 30 years ago, the standard of living in China has been continuously increasing. In the past few years, the proportion of resident income in national income has steadily reduced. The proportion of labor income in primary distribution and household consumption rates, as well as Chinese families' Engel's coefficient also dropped slowly, which influenced the growth of domestic consumption. Unceasing enhancement of residential income and consumption level is very important not only to expand consumption and transform the development path but also for people to maintain positive economic psychology and thus sustain stable development.

(3) Straightening out income distribution order

The adjustment of income distribution should be regarded as a strategic measure to expand domestic demand, to enhance standard of living, to promote common prosperity, and to maintain social harmony and stability. To adjust the income distribution structure, the proportional relations between the payment for labor and capital revenue in primary distribution should be straightened out, the proportional relations among the income of the country, enterprises, and people in the national income should be straightened out; some levers such as finance, tax revenue, social security, and social welfare should play a bigger role in the normalization of redistribution, and the development of philanthropy should be vigorously pushed.

(4) Maintaining social harmony and stability

Social harmony and stability are the foundations of development. Due to rapid advancements of system reform and structural transformation, different development phases within China coexist and various contradictions interweave, in particular, the income differential unceasingly has expanded, which has become a cause for some social problems. Therefore, these problems should be emphatically solved in reform and development; the development demands of various aspects should be planned as a whole, and interest relations between various social classes and strata should be coordinated. The middle-income group should be more empowered, the low-income group should be reduced, and the impoverished should receive aid. Historical problems caused because of the restructuring of enterprise, home relocation, land expropriation, immigration, and environmental pollution should be solved thoroughly to push the thorough settlement of social contradictions, ultimately favoring the maintenance of social harmony and stability.

(5) Emphatically implementing comprehensive social reform

China's economic reform has provided strong social power for development. The goal of social reform is to unceasingly provide a powerful engine for development of all forms. The expansion of income differential should be reversed through the adjustment of income distribution structures — mass consumption should be cultivated, and economic growth should be supported by domestic demand. A management system that adapts to the market economy and modern population movement should be established through social management systems, such as reform of household registry in order to guarantee social harmony and stability. Nonprofit systems that effectively operate to serve the public welfare should be established through the reform of medical institutions, the educational system, and cultural organizations. The

social safety network should cover all people through the development
and consummation of the social security system in order to stabilize
consumption and build a social security system for families to dodge
the risks of a market economy and social change.

VI. Data and Methodology

The main data source for this book's research and analysis came from the
"Chinese Social Survey 2008" (CSS 2008, CASS) conducted by the
Institute of Sociology at the Chinese Academy of Social Sciences. The
Chinese Social Survey(CSS), a large-scale project of longitudinal surveys,
aims to gather data on social change in the reforming period of Chinese
society. This survey provides complete, accurate, and scientific foundation
regarding information for the research of social science and governmental
policy-making.

The subject of the 2008 survey was "the people's livelihood", and was
carried in 135 countries (city, district, borough) of 28 provinces (autonomous region, municipality) from May to September 2008; the design
sample size was 7,001 and 7,139 successful questionnaires were taken
back. Here, the survey design and the implementation step are explained
as follows.

A. *Sampling design and procedure*

The sampling design of the CSS 2008 was basically consistent with its
predecessor, the first wave survey in 2006. All people aged between
18 and 69 years were regarded as the overall sample to be included in this
survey. The survey used the method of multistage composed sampling,
namely five-stage sampling of county (city, district, borough), township
(town/street), villagers' (urban residents') committee, household, and resident; each stage adopted different sampling methods (see Table 1). The
sampling frame of CSS 2008 basically followed the one of CSS 2006.

Sampling units of (city, district, borough) in stage I were sampled
based on "Data of Counties in Census 2000" in the Fifth National Census
and 130 primary sampling units (PSU) were drawn out of total 2,797
counties (city, district, borough) via the stratified proportional sampling.

Table 1. Sampling Design and Distribution of Multistage Sampling Units.

Sampling phase	Sampling unit PSU	Quantity	Sampling method
Phase I	County city, (district, borough)	130	Stratified proportional sampling + PPS sampling
Phase II	Township (town/street)	260	PPS sampling
Phase III	Villagers' (urban residents') committee	520	PPS sampling
Phase IV	Household	7,001	Equidistant sampling
Phase V	Resident	7,001	Simple random sampling

Note: PPS: probability proportional to size.

In detail, firstly, 2797 counties (city, district, borough) were clustered into 37 strata according to seven variables of four indicators, including the urban population proportion, the age, the education level, and the industrial proportion (see Table 2). Secondly, counties (city, district, borough) were sampled from each stratum through probability proportional to size (PPS) method. Then a total of 130 counties (city, district borough) were sampled, which covered 28 provinces (autonomous region/municipality) (see Figure 6).

In stage II, the frame comprises township (town/street) list, including their roll of household and residents in population statistics, which were provided by the related departments of counties (city, district, borough) sampled in the first-stage. From each country (city, district, borough), two townships (town/street) were sampled by the PPS method, and there were a total of 260 samples.

In stage III, the frame comprises list of villagers' (urban residents') committees, including their roll of population statistics, which were provided by the related departments of townships (town/street) sampled in the second-stage. From each township, two villagers' (urban residents') committees were sampled by the PPS method, and there were a total of 520 samples.

In stage IV, the households were sampled by systematic sampling, but the detailed steps were different from the first wave 2006 survey. First, it unified the method of household roll sampling with regional address

Table 2. Distribution of Sampling Units of Various Stratifications and Sample Size.

East						Central						West					
Stratification number	Number of cities, counties, and districts	Proportion of population aged 15 years and above	Number of cities, counties, and districts sampled	Sample number of villagers' (urban residents') committees	Sample number of various stratifications	Stratification number	Number of cities, counties, and districts	Proportion of population aged 15 years old and above	Number of cities, counties, and districts sampled	Sample number of villagers' (urban residents') committees	Sample number of various stratifications	Stratification number	Number of cities, counties, and districts	Proportion of population aged 15 years old and above	Number of cities, counties, and districts sampled	Sample number of villagers' (urban residents') committees	Sample number of various stratifications
1	98	13.07	6	26	613	1	110	5.51	3	35	284	1	76	10.06	4	15	242
2	72	11.42	6	14	343	2	34	2.48	2	22	173	2	72	7	2	18	140
3	63	10.78	4	11	179	3	71	4.15	2	31	252	3	125	12.42	4	11	178
4	63	7.61	4	10	155	4	71	5.61	2	16	130	4	94	14.13	4	12	193
5	26	2.88	2	8	65	5	68	10.24	6	10	233	5	98	10.66	4	13	216
6	77	12.68	6	7	161	6	84	8	5	10	160	6	59	6.76	2	14	111
7	69	7.80	5	11	175	7	78	7.13	4	11	182	7	76	8.85	2	15	124
8	38	5.57	3	35	278	8	109	6.09	4	14	230	8	115	13.04	4	12	193
9	67	8.93	4	10	157	9	65	5.87	2	18	143	9	99	5.71	2	12	95
10	45	5.78	2	20	157	10	73	6.16	4	10	156	10	79	11.38	4	10	153

(Continued)

Table 2. (*Continued*).

East

Stratification number	Number of cities, counties, and districts	Proportion of population aged 15 years and above	Number of cities, counties, and districts sampled	Sample number of villagers' (urban residents') committees	Sample number of various stratifications
11	82	13.49	6	10	234
Total 700		100	48	–	2,518

Central

Stratification number	Number of cities, counties, and districts	Proportion of population aged 15 years old and above	Number of cities, counties, and districts sampled	Sample number of villagers' (urban residents') committees	Sample number of various stratifications
11	98	6.97	4	12	193
12	85	8.42	4	10	158
13	85	7.22	5	11	182
14	64	6.73	4	10	156
15	62	5.29	2	16	130
16	47	4.14	2	10	79
Total 1,204		100	55	–	2,838

West

Stratification number	Number of cities, counties, and districts	Proportion of population aged 15 years old and above	Number of cities, counties, and districts sampled	Sample number of villagers' (urban residents') committees	Sample number of various stratifications
Total 893		100	32	–	1,645

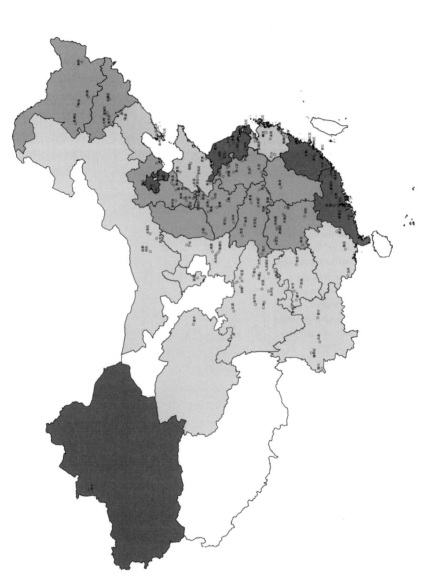

Figure 6. Distribution of Sampling Frame of 130 Cities, Counties, and Districts in General Survey of Chinese Society in 2006–2008.

sampling. As it is difficult for the floating population to be covered in the household roll of villagers' (urban residents') committees in survey sites, address sampling was employed in all villagers' (urban residents') committees sampled. Area maps were firstly drawn including all buildings under the jurisdiction of village/residents' committees, then the household addresses were listed to form an optional sampling frame. When the original household roll did not reflect the actual housing situation of the population of villagers' (urban residents') committees, the address sampling would be used. Second, some stipulations were given to household sampling concerning multiple households at a single address, namely each household at an address was given a serial number, and we sampled a household to visit with a random selection. With respect to the collective households where several people lived together without family relation (such as dormitory of enterprise staffs), a room was regarded as an independent household and was sampled within the random table.

In the last phase, interviewers visited interviewees in their homes. After entering households, interviewers first recorded all household residents' information in "Registration Form for Household Residents", then eligible family members were selected according to the following requirements (the lower and the upper limits of interviewees' age are 18 and 69, moreover interviewees have lived or will live in the household for at least one week). The eligible members were then sorted into "Kish Grid" according to the sex and age order "Kish Grid", with its eight selection tables in the correct proportion , is capable of selecting an interviewee out of eligible family members with equal selection probabilities (see Table 3). Regarding the collective household, the information of all people in this household was recorded in the "Collective Household Population Registration Form" and the acceptable interviewees were selected with the random table.

B. *Training of supervisors/interviewers*

To guarantee the quality of the field survey, we entrusted a professional survey organization to implement the survey and manage interviewers. A total of 366 interviewers, 82 supervisors, and 13 inspectors participated in visitation, management, and supervision. To gather survey data under the control of standard flow, we referenced the *Interviewer Training Handbook*

Table 3. Registration Form for Household Residents and KISH Grid.

Registration Form for Household Resident					KISH Grid									
Quantity	X1 Relation with answerer	X2 Sex	X3 Age	X4 Visiting	No.	Sex	Age	Y1	Y2	Y3				
1	Answerer				1	1	1	1	1	1	1	1	1	1
2					2	1	1	1	2	2	2	2	2	2
3					3	1	1	2	2	3	3	3	3	3
4					4	1	2	2	3	3	3	4	4	4
5					5	1	2	2	3	3	4	5	5	5
6					6	1	2	3	4	4	5	5	5	6
7					7	1	2	3	4	5	5	5	5	6
8					8	1	2	3	4	5	5	6	5	6

of the Survey Research Center at the University of Michigan and formulated approximately a four- to five-day training course consisting of eight units, including the project background and the explanation of the operation plan, studying *Interviewer Training Handbook*, the record of visiting registration forms, the address sampling and visiting interviewees, filling in the questionnaire and explanations, coding, analog visiting practices, and pilot surveys. The unified training was a requirement for all interviewers and field supervisors who participated in the field work so that they could maintain a professional role in the survey. All training materials were made into a video to guarantee the same standard of training at each survey site. Trainees included interviewers, supervisors, and inspectors.

For the interviewer, the training taught them how to complete the visit to the interviewees, the field interview, checking questionnaires, and thereafter coding. For this purpose, we provided an *Interviewer's Handbook* for interviewers, which it explained in detail the use of visiting sampling tools.

Supervisor mainly took charge of the technical guidance and quality control in the survey, including the household sampling, the questionnaire assignment, replacing families visited and interviewees, checking questionnaires, organizing coding work, and so on. Except for the training of interviewers, supervisor also accepted special training in the field of address sampling, household sampling, households sampled, and replacing interviewees and questionnaire inspections.

Inspectors mainly observed and supervised whether supervisors and interviewers implemented the survey according to the standards of the survey plan. As requested, inspectors recorded the entire survey process in the form of *Log Books* every day, and reported the survey progress to the task group day after day. To guarantee the independence of supervision functions, inspectors were composed of members of a task group, the Chinese Academy of Social Sciences, and masters and doctors who had nothing to do with survey organization.

The survey training consisted of two levels of training, the task group members first carried out the overall project training to local supervisors and inspectors in Beijing, and then supervisors went to various areas to train interviewers. All interviewers and supervisors who were trained and passed the examination were required to wear the card of interviewers issued by the Chinese Academy of Social Sciences.

C. *Survey implementation*

To guarantee quality control in the field survey, the survey used methods of work of "field groups", namely surveys of each of the villagers' (urban residents') committees was completed together by one to two supervisors and five to ten interviewers. Each group would complete the survey of the villagers' (urban residents') committees in about two to seven days; interviewers visited sites for 1 to 1.5 hours on average. After finishing the survey of a site, the "field group" would move to the next survey site. This kind of operating mode is intended to solve possible problems in the survey. Moreover, because of the joint work of supervisors and interviewers, nonstandard visiting was eliminated to the greatest degree. The detailed flow of visiting is as follows:

In the first step, the supervisor assigns interviewers the questionnaires according to the sampling list of the villagers' (urban residents') committees. To control visiting quality, the official questionnaire is provided to interviewers at the survey site and taken back, and issued again one by one. In this way, the possible visiting error cannot be expanded.

In the second step, interviewers hold the sampling list, the sampling table, and the questionnaire to choose interviewees in the households surveyed. If sampling is smooth, the visit continues, but if sampling fails, the supervisor should be informed to report to the center of task group, and to receive the list of backup households visited in order to replace a failed sample so that the sampling can be carried out once again. If the difference between the initial and the actual situation is significant, the supervisor will identify the circumstances to the task group. After the circumstances are confirmed by the task group, the field address sampling may be carried. After the field sampling drawing and the detailed enumeration of sampling addresses are completed, the supervisor should return the complete sampling information to the task group, and the task group returns to the address sampled to conduct the survey.

In the third step, after confirming the interviewee's preferred time and carrying on the access environment control, the interviewer begins the interview. The questionnaire is held by the interviewer throughout, and the interviewer asks the questions one by one and records the answers. The interviewee answers the questions one by one. The interviewee cannot fill in the questionnaire, except for few questions and also cannot see the content of questionnaire.

In the fourth step, after the visit is complete, the interviewer confirms whether any answers to the questionnaire were omitted, mistaken, ambiguous, or contradictory; then, they express their appreciation to the interviewee after confirming no mistakes and sign and hand in the questionnaire.

In the fifth step, the supervisor takes back the questionnaire that the interviewer hands in at the site and checks it. If there are no mistakes, the supervisor provides the questionnaire for the next address; if a mistake is found, the supervisor should immediately make the interviewer return to the family visited. All questionnaires entered the coding flow only after the interviewer and supervisor have double-checked its accuracy.

To strengthen the field control and guarantee the quality of the visit, the following measures were also taken in the survey: (i) access time was limited. To guarantee all members of the family visited are selected, the survey time for urban residents was arranged for the weekend or after work (6:00 to 9:30 pm); most rural residents had the limited working time, and the visiting time for them was not limited. (ii) Supervisor accompanies interviewer on the visit. To guarantee that the interviewer had correctly carried out visiting regulations, the supervisor accompanies the interviewer during 10% of each interviewer's total visiting time so as to correct the mistakes promptly. (iii) Visiting was checked with the return receipt. When the survey ended, interviewees were given a return receipt, where some key aspects of the visit were inquired about, with postage stamp, and interviewee had to mail it back to the task group after filling it in. (iv) The task group provided technical support. The task group is set up by the duty officer during the survey implementation to carry out technical guidance and management of the survey in various areas by telephone. The main work of the task group was to check the replacement of samples. According to the survey regulations, the duty officer must provide the backup list to replace samples; interviewers or supervisor could not replace samples.

D. *Implementation time and the progress*

The design sample size of this survey was 7,001 persons, but in the process of actual address sampling, we discovered that many floating populations in some villagers' (urban residents') committees were not covered in the original sampling frame; therefore, some samples were supplemented. As a result, the sample size in this survey ultimately included 7,139 questionnaires. Among them, the sample size for urban and rural areas was 3,629 and 3,510 questionnaires, respectively. It covered 28 provinces/municipalities, in which master sample size was 7,001 questionnaires and 138 were supplemented (3 questionnaires in Sichuan, 80 in Guangdong, and 55 in Fujian).

The survey was implemented in three batches: the first batch was done from May 26 to July 20, 2008, the implementation area was 13 provinces (municipalities): Hunan, Henan, Beijing, Guangdong, Shanxi, Shanghai, Tianjin, Jiangsu, Zhejiang, Hubei, Heilongjiang, Jilin, and Hebei and consisted of 4,449 questionnaires; the second batch was done from June 15 to July 30, the implementation area was 14 provinces (autonomous regions): Fujian, Liaoning, Shandong, Guizhou, Inner Mongolia, Jiangxi, Anhui, Shanxi, Yunnan, Guangxi, Xinjiang, Qinghai, and Ningxia and consisted of 1,834 questionnaires. As a result of influence of Wenchuan earthquake in May 2008, the survey progress in southwest area was postponed and from August 10 to September 5 the survey in Sichuan and Chongqing was completed, and there were 718 questionnaires.

E. *Date checking*

In the survey, multiple checking was selected to guarantee the accuracy of questionnaire information. (i) Interviewers checked at the site whether the questionnaire was qualified; (ii) supervisors checked all questionnaires at site for a second time; (iii) the local executing organization at random selected 30% of questionnaires completed to make telephone calls to verify the surveys; (iv) the survey organization checked all questionnaires for the third time in Beijing; (v) the task group independently checked 10% of questionnaires in Beijing. The content checked included whether an interviewee was at the household that its address was sampled at; whether some data, such as the answers to the questions about age and occupation, were consistent with reality; whether deep logical relations between the questions was reasonable; whether there was omission; whether the codes were correct; whether the data was mistakenly included;

whether to ask questions in certain aspects in visiting; how long the visits were; and whether they received the return receipt.

The checking of statistical results indicated that a total of 2,565 questionnaires were paid a return visit after survey ended, which occupied 36.9% of 7,139 questionnaires taken back. The qualified questionnaire after checking accounted for 87.4% of the total, and there were only a small amount of wrong samplings (3.37% of "incorrect interviewee"), and the wrong enumeration of family members (3.26%), as well as another 12.6% of unqualified questionnaires.

A total of 7,139 return receipts were provided along with 7,139 effective questionnaires, and finally took back 5,230 receipts, returns ratio of which was 73.26%.

F. *Data processing and weighting*

A total of 7,139 qualified questionnaires were included in the survey database. This data was verified and straightened out twice successively with the verification of frequency analysis and variable connection. This data was contrasted with the results and the cruising data in the sampling survey of 1% population in 2005 by the National Bureau of Statistics to make weighing processes.

First is weighting of data by separating urban and rural populations. In the initial sample assignment, while designing the sampling, considering the urban social structure was more complex, the rural social structure had more homogeneity. We enlarged the proportion of urban sample (the urban sample accounted for 54.1%, and rural sample 45.9%); in other words, there were sampling designs that gave different probabilities to urban and rural populations; therefore, the cruising data was given weight afterward according to the result of the sampling survey to a population of 1% in 2005 (see Table 4).

Second is the weighting of population by different age groups and sexes. The cruising data after weighting to the proportion of the above-mentioned urban and rural population was further contrasted with the basic variables of the data of the sampling survey to a population of 1% in 2005. Because there was a three-year gap between the 2008 survey and the 2005 sampling survey, the comparison of age groups was shifted forward three

Table 4. Distribution of Urban and Rural Populations in the 2008 Survey and in the Sampling Survey of 1% Population in 2005 and Weighting Result.

| | Sampling survey of 1% population in 2005 | | Survey in 2008 | | | | | |
| | Proportion of urban population | Proportion of rural population | Urban population | Rural population | Weighting of urban population | Weighting of rural population | Urban population after weighting | Rural population after weighting |
Age in 2008	A	B	c	d	a/(c/(c+d))	d/(d/(c+d))		
18	0.36789	0.63211	22	29	0.85282	1.11165	19	32
19	0.40126	0.59874	51	50	0.79465	1.20946	41	60
20	0.44726	0.55274	41	43	0.91633	1.07977	38	46
21	0.47621	0.52379	43	32	0.83060	1.22763	36	39
22	0.49301	0.50699	51	31	0.79269	1.34106	40	42
23	0.49558	0.50442	41	26	0.80985	1.29986	33	34
24	0.50676	0.49324	42	32	0.89286	1.14062	38	36
25	0.51480	0.48520	50	34	0.86486	1.19874	43	41
26	0.52349	0.47651	59	32	0.80742	1.35507	48	43
27	0.51730	0.48270	56	34	0.83137	1.27775	47	43
28	0.51328	0.48672	43	39	0.97882	1.02335	42	40
29	0.53049	0.46951	58	37	0.86891	1.20549	50	45

(Continued)

Table 4. (*Continued*).

| Age in 2008 | Sampling survey of 1% population in 2005 | | Survey in 2008 | | | | | |
| | Proportion of urban population | Proportion of rural population | Urban population | Rural population | Weighting of urban population | Weighting of rural population | Urban population after weighting | Rural population after weighting |
	A	B	c	d	$a/(c/(c+d))$	$d/(d/(c+d))$		
30	0.53202	0.46798	69	33	0.78646	1.44649	54	48
31	0.53093	0.46907	63	38	0.85117	1.24675	54	47
32	0.52861	0.47139	54	51	1.02785	0.97051	56	49
33	0.52333	0.47667	73	40	0.81008	1.34660	59	54
34	0.51170	0.48830	77	46	0.81739	1.30567	63	60
35	0.51526	0.48474	86	58	0.86277	1.20348	74	70
36	0.50967	0.49033	95	98	1.03544	0.96565	98	95
37	0.50457	0.49543	110	90	0.91740	1.10096	101	99
38	0.49354	0.50646	120	109	0.94183	1.06404	113	116
39	0.48742	0.51258	82	109	1.13534	0.89819	93	98
40	0.47769	0.52231	151	132	0.89528	1.11980	135	148
41	0.45408	0.54592	85	89	0.92952	1.06731	79	95
42	0.45829	0.54171	73	130	1.27441	0.84591	93	110
43	0.46994	0.53006	102	130	1.06887	0.94596	109	123

(*Continued*)

Table 4. (*Continued*).

| Age in 2008 | Sampling survey of 1% population in 2005 | | Survey in 2008 | | | | | |
	Proportion of urban population A	Proportion of rural population B	Urban population c	Rural population d	Weighting of urban population a/(c/(c+d))	Weighting of rural population d/(d/(c+d))	Urban population after weighting	Rural population after weighting
44	0.48211	0.51789	88	118	1.12859	0.90410	99	107
45	0.49291	0.50709	166	126	0.86705	1.17515	144	148
46	0.47231	0.52769	116	112	0.92833	1.07423	108	120
47	0.48383	0.51617	72	55	0.85342	1.19188	61	66
48	0.49226	0.50774	67	63	0.95512	1.04773	64	66
49	0.48818	0.51182	61	55	0.92833	1.07948	57	59
50	0.47236	0.52764	95	83	0.88505	1.13157	84	94
51	0.45724	0.54276	98	89	0.87250	1.14040	86	101
52	0.45026	0.54974	93	82	0.84726	1.17323	79	96
53	0.44013	0.55987	102	76	0.76806	1.31128	78	100
54	0.44473	0.55527	99	77	0.79063	1.26919	78	98
55	0.42955	0.57045	91	70	0.75997	1.31204	69	92
56	0.42469	0.57531	97	90	0.81874	1.19536	79	108
57	0.42563	0.57437	75	73	0.83991	1.16448	63	85

(*Continued*)

Table 4. (*Continued*).

Age in 2008	Sampling survey of 1% population in 2005		Survey in 2008					
	Proportion of urban population	Proportion of rural population	Urban population	Rural population	Weighting of urban population	Weighting of rural population	Urban population after weighting	Rural population after weighting
	A	B	c	d	$a/(c/(c+d))$	$d/(d/(c+d))$		
58	0.42380	0.57620	76	57	0.74165	1.34447	56	77
59	0.42294	0.57706	84	64	0.74518	1.33445	63	85
60	0.41683	0.58317	75	61	0.75586	1.30017	57	79
61	0.41787	0.58213	48	43	0.79221	1.23195	38	53
62	0.41793	0.58207	64	38	0.66607	1.56241	43	59
63	0.40701	0.59299	48	45	0.78858	1.22552	38	55
64	0.40805	0.59195	51	36	0.69609	1.43054	36	51
65	0.40913	0.59087	42	41	0.80852	1.19615	34	49
66	0.42231	0.57769	52	34	0.69844	1.46121	36	50
67	0.42227	0.57773	75	38	0.63622	1.71798	48	65
68	0.42196	0.57804	68	42	0.68259	1.51391	46	64
69	0.43235	0.56765	62	37	0.69037	1.51884	43	56
			3862	3277			3341	3798
Total proportion	0.470	0.530	0.541	0.459			0.468	0.532

years; namely, the proportion of population aged 18 years in 2008 should be compared with the group aged 15 years in the 2005 sampling survey. The distribution of populations of different age groups and sexes showed that, compared with the sampling survey, the proportion of the population in the 18- to 34-year-old group in the General Survey of Chinese Society in 2008 was somewhat lower, but the proportion in the 50-year-old and above group was somewhat high; the proportion of woman was high, while the proportion of men was somewhat lower (see Table 5, Figure 7).

On one hand, because we carried on the visiting survey in a fixed time cycle (generally the access schedule did not surpass seven days in a survey site), the actual survey aimed at those populations that lived at home during the survey. Generally speaking, young people and men were more likely than old people to not be at home; thus, the probability that young people and men were selected was somewhat lower. On the other hand, because the acquisition of data from the original sampling survey was different from our actual survey, the information of family members in the sampling survey did not indicate that other people surveyed were at home at the time

Table 5. Distribution of Different Age Groups and Sexes in CGSS 2008 and in the Sampling Survey of 1% Population in 2005.

		Proportion of sampling survey of 1% population	Proportion of CGSS survey
Age groups (years)	18 to 24	13.11	6.28
	25 to 29	9.45	6.08
	30 to 34	12.31	9.90
	35 to 39	14.06	14.04
	40 to 44	12.56	15.25
	45 to 49	9.77	10.63
	50 to 54	10.53	12.85
	55 to 59	7.72	10.27
	60 to 64	5.69	7.84
	65 to 69	4.80	6.87
Sex	Man	49.74	46.32
	Woman	50.26	53.68

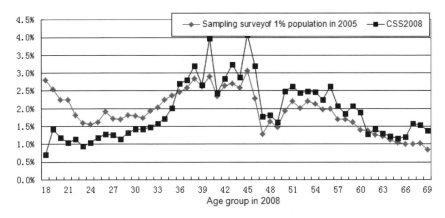

Figure 7. Distribution of age groups in the 2008 survey and in the sampling survey of 1% population in 2005.

of the survey. Our survey obtained information data of individuals who were actually on the scene, so the data of the two surveys was inevitably different. The proportion of younger age groups and men was somewhat low, which was universal for the visiting survey in the set time; therefore, we regarded it as a system error, and noted that it needed to be corrected by weighting.

According to the above comparative analysis regarding the interactive classifications of three variables in urban and rural populations, and with sex and age in the 2005 sampling survey as the weighting standard, the cruising data of the 2008 survey was given the comprehensive weighting. After weighting, the result is as follows (see Table 6):

It can be seen that the data adjusted by weighting in area, gender, and age is consistent with the result of the sampling survey from 2005. In terms of educational level, except the proportion with an educational level of junior high school, there was a difference of almost 8%. The results in other classifications are also extremely approximate. Therefore, this cruising data may be used to conclude about all of China including urban and rural residents, as well as residents from the east, central, and west.

Table 6. Characteristics of Populations in the 2008 Survey and in the Sampling Survey of 1% Population in 2005 After Weighting.

		Proportion of sampling survey of 1% population	Proportion of CGSS
Area	Urban area	46.98	46.98
	Rural area	53.02	53.02
Sex	Man	50.89	49.91
	Woman	49.10	50.01
	18 to 24	14.83	14.83
	25 to 29	8.76	8.76
	30 to 34	9.76	9.76
	35 to 39	12.89	12.89
	40 to 44	13.19	13.19
Age group (years)	45 to 49	9.76	9.76
	50 to 54	10.51	10.51
	55 to 59	8.99	8.99
	60 to 64	6.36	6.36
	65 to 69	4.94	4.94
	Uneducated	7.35	9.72
	Elementary school	27.64	24.31
	Junior high school	43.06	34.92
Educational level	Senior high school	14.49	19.66
	Junior college	4.86	6.79
	University	2.42	4.31
	Master	0.19	0.30

Chapter 1

The People's Livelihood in China

Li Peilin and Li Wei

The Report to the 17th National Congress of the Communist Party of China made important decisions and stressed the necessity to "speed up social construction based on the improvement of the people's livelihood". In recent years, in the domains of employment, income distribution, social security, education, medical service, housing, and environmental protection, safeguarding and improving people's livelihood has assumed importance. A series of related social policies has been put into practice, and people have obtained actual benefits, which has played an influential role in improving the people's livelihood and in promoting social stability.

At present, China has entered a developmental phase that promotes industrial agriculture and drives rural development by corresponding urban development as a whole. China has entered an important period in which they have put forth efforts to eradicate the urban and rural dualistic structures and to form a new pattern of integration in terms of urban and rural economic and social development. In this period, the people's livelihood, as compared with the initial period of reform and opening up, has undergone drastic changes. With the enhancement of material and cultural demands, people's livelihood has taken on a more widespread meaning than having enough food and clothing and people's desires now reflect new demands in terms of quality of life and the living environment, as well as the construction of the people's livelihood in the process of swift economic growth.

To understand the people's livelihood and the ensuing problems at present, as well as the public opinion on the construction of people's livelihood, the Institute of Sociology at the Chinese Academy of Social Sciences carried out the the second wave of "Chinese Social Survey" in 2008 (CSS 2008)[1] from May to September 2008. This national sampling survey covered 135 counties (city, district), 257 townships (town, street), and 520 villagers' (urban residents') committees in 28 provinces, municipalities, and autonomous regions, which included a total 7,139 residents aged between 18 and 69 years with a survey error smaller than 2%, which met the scientific requirements of statistical inference.[2] Based on this cruising data and the first survey data in 2006, this research report was made.

---

[1] "Survey of Chinese Society", the important project of the Chinese Academy of Social Sciences about the survey of national conditions, was a large survey and research to the entire society that the Institute of Sociology of the Chinese Academy of Social Sciences took charge and covered 130 counties (cities, districts), 260 townships (town, street) and 520 villagers'/urban residents' committees in 28 provinces, which can conclude all residents as a whole. Survey is done once every two years, and the first survey was done from April to August 2006. The second survey in 2008 was sponsored by the Ministry of Civil Affairs of China and local departments of civil affairs, which the authors acknowledge here.

[2] In accordance with strict scientific sampling methods, the sampling frame was designed based on the statistical data of counties (cities, districts) in the Fifth National Census in 2000, and the stratified, multi-stage sampling method was used. First, four indicators, namely the proportion of urban population, age, education level, and industrial scale and seven variables were used in 2,797 districts, cities, and counties in the east, middle, and west to carry on the clustering stratification. The PPS method was used to sample 135 districts, cities, and counties in 37 stratifications and was also used to sample two townships/towns/street in every district, city, and county sampled. In every township/town/street sampled, the PPS method was used to sample two villagers'/urban residents' committees, and then the list of all individuals or households was gathered in the villagers'/urban residents' committees sampled, which covered more than 1.6 million people, and nearly 500,000 families. And then, in this sampling frame, PPS method was used to sample all individuals or families, and finally 7,001 families were sampled to carry on the visiting survey. As for floating populations that increased newly in the survey sites, we made the necessary supplements, therefore the final sample size was 7,139.

I. Urban and Rural Residents' Living Conditions

A. *Residents' living conditions have been largely improved, but the income differential is still obvious*

Of the urban and rural residents, 70% thought that living standards had improved. The survey results showed that whether in the subjective sensation or in objective income, all subjects reflected that the living conditions have improved. Nearly 70% of urban and rural residents believed that their living standard was better than that five years ago and only 12.4% of urban and rural residents thought that their living standard had declined. Nearly 60% of urban and rural residents believed that, over the next five years, the living condition would continue to improve. This not only reflected people's full affirmation of economic development and the improvement of living conditions but also indicated positive anticipation for the future (see Table 1.1).

As compared with the data of the first "General Survey of Chinese Society" (in 2006), it is observed that, in 2008, the urban and rural residents had a stronger sense of profiting in the economy. The proportion of population that thought the living standards were better was up 6% from 2006, and those who had optimistic anticipation of the improvement in living standard in next five years had grown by 4.4%.

Table 1.1.   Urban and Rural Residents' Appraisal to Living Condition (in 2006, in 2008).

Question: As compared with five years ago, your living standard is …			Question: After five years, you feel your living standard will …		
Answer	In 2008	In 2006	Answer	In 2008	In 2006
Better and better	13.6	9.7	Better and better	11.8	10.6
A little better	55.8	53.7	A little better	46.5	43.3
No change	17.7	22.1	No change	17.3	17
A little worse	9.3	9	A little worse	7	6.8
Worse and worse	3.1	4.9	Worse and worse	1.7	2.7
Hard to tell	0.5	0.6	Hard to tell	15.7	19.6
Sample number	7,139	7,061	Sample number	7,139	7,061

Note: Unit: %.

Further analysis indicated that, since 2006, rural residents had obviously more of a sense of improvement than urban residents. In Figure 1.1, we see that in the first survey conducted in 2006, the proportion of rural residents that thought the living standard had improved was 69%, which was higher by nearly 13% than urban residents at same time. In the second survey, in 2008, the proportion rose to 76.3%, which was still higher by 13% compared to the urban residents at same time. This tendency showed that, since 2006, a series of policies on strengthening agriculture, benefitting farmers, helping farmers, and enriching rural areas, including cancelling the agricultural tax, direct grain subsidy, generalizing new rural cooperative medical service, carrying out rural free compulsory education, and promoting the rural social security, was implemented so that rural residents could benefit from it.

The survey indicated that the quality of life has been unceasingly improving, and the proportion of expenditures on food consumption was gradually reducing. According to the cruising data, urban and rural families' Engel's coefficient was 35.2% in 2007, and nearly 78% of families' living standards had reached a "well-off" level. According to the related international standards, the households in which the living standard reached an Engel coefficient value below 30% accounted for 39.1%, those that reached an Engel's coefficient of 30–39% accounted for 20.8%, those that reached an Engel's coefficient of 40–49% accounted for 18%, and the families with an Engel's coefficient of 50% above accounted for 22.1% of the total.

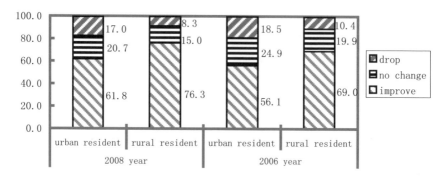

Figure 1.1. Urban and Rural Residents' Appraisal to the Change of Living Condition for 5 Years (in 2006, in 2008).

The real estate conditions have also largely improved. The cruising data indicated that the per capita living space was 42.8 m^2 (with a median of 30 m^2), and rural per capita living space amounted to 49.8 m^2 (with a median of 36 m^2).[3] The estimated value of families interviewed to own real estate was RMB 158,000/household on average, in which large or medium-sized city residents' estimate value of real estate was RMB 295,000/household on average, whereas that of small urban residents was approximately RMB 162,000/household, and for rural residents, it was RMB 90,000/household. This scenario indicated that the overwhelming majority of residents' housing conditions had underwent great improvement, and that real estate had become an important and basic property of urban and rural families (see Table 1.2).

We should also note that the real estate conditions and housing conditions had big differentials in urban and rural areas and under different household incomes. The housing conditions of low-income families, particularly those in large or medium-sized cities, largely fell behind other groups. The proportion of home owners in large or medium-sized urban families in which per capita income belonged to the low level was about 80%, which was 10% lower than the average level of large or medium-sized cities; per capita housing area was also about 20 m^2, which was lower than the average level by approximately 10 m^2. Therefore, for mid- and low-income families living in large or medium-sized cities, the improvement of housing conditions is a big concern.

Bigger differentials of income distribution restricted personal consumption. Although urban and rural residents' living standards have greatly improved in the past two years, the expansion of income differential was still clear. In 2007, the average household income of 20% of urban and rural families' per capita income, the highest income group was more 17.1 times than 20%

---

[3] According to *China Statistical Yearbook 2008*, urban per capita building area was 27.1 m^2 (2006), and rural per capita housing space 31.6 m^2 (2007), which had a large difference from our survey result. We must explain this: (1) there was a difference in target limitation. We used usable floor area in the survey, and contained courtyard in the rural area; (2) there was a difference in computing mode. The computing mode of urban per capita building area in the *Statistical Yearbook* was from gross urban building area to be divided by the number of urban populations, which was different from our computing mode of own housing as a unit.

Table 1.2. Housing Condition Under Urban and Rural Areas and Different Household Incomes.

		Per capita living space (m^2)	Value of house (RMB 10,000)
Whole		**42.8**	**15.8**
Large and	**Total**	**29.6**	**29.5**
medium-sized city	Least 20%	19.1	10.5
	Lower 20%	20.6	13.4
	Medium 20%	23.2	19.4
	Higher 20%	26.2	23.1
	Highest 20%	36.6	41.7
Small city	**Total**	**41.7**	**16.2**
	Least 20%	32.6	8.1
	Lower 20%	38.8	10
	Medium 20%	37.6	14.3
	Higher 20%	41.6	16.4
	Highest 20%	57.6	31.6
Rural area	**Total**	**49.8**	**9**
	Least 20%	40.3	5.5
	Lower 20%	47	7.1
	Medium 20%	54.4	9.9
	Higher 20%	55.2	10.5
	Highest 20%	73.8	24

lowest income group. The income differential between regions was also obvious; the east's average household income was 2.03 times and 1.98 times more than west and central areas, respectively (see Table 1.3).

An immediate consequence of income differential expansion is to restrict mid- and low-income families' consumption. Through the data in Table 1.4, we may see that, in the possession rate of consumer durable goods, the difference between high- and low-income households is obvious. Taking the refrigerator as an example, 87.5% of families in the highest income group have a refrigerator, as compared to 22.75% in the lowest income group; as for large-scale goods, mobile phones are used widely in the highest income group (possession rate is 96.4%), but in the lowest income families, there is only a 64% possession rate; in terms of personal computers, the differential is

Table 1.3. Distribution and Differential of Families' Per Capita Annual Income.

	Families' per capita annual income (RMB)	Ratio between 20% of highest income group and 20% of lowest income group	Sample size
Whole	**8,282.57**	**17.1:1**	**6,741**
East	12,130.54	13.8:1	2,463
Central	6,124.11	11.6:1	2,658
West	5,972.60	17:1	1,620
Urban area	11,550.27	12.6:1	3,225
Rural area	5,284.67[a]	13:1	3,516

Note: The household income for farming in rural household income was calculated by not deducting gross income of input cost; therefore, rural residents' actual net income is lower.

Table 1.4. Possession Rate of Consumer Durable Goods in Different Income Groups.

	Sample size	Color TV	Refrigerator	Washing machine	Handset	Microwave oven	PC	Car	Camcorder
20% of the highest income families	1,314	98.5	87.5	89.09	96.39	60.36	66.37	18.79	15.66
20% of higher income families	1,249	97.81	72.37	76.11	91.7	29.95	32.44	6.01	4.88
20% of mid-income families	1,375	96.36	56.07	66.05	87.29	16.4	18.43	4.99	1.33
20% of lower income families	1,425	93.93	37.57	57.28	77.12	9.33	6.97	2.69	0.67
20% of the lowest income families	1,378	84.01	22.75	41.69	63.77	3.95	3.97	2.53	0.47

Note: Unit: %.

more obvious, nearly two-third of families in the highest income group have a computer, but less than 4% of families in the lowest income group have one. Therefore, it is pivotal in terms of domestic demand to reduce the income differential and enhance the incomes of the mid- and low-income stratum.

B. *Pressure in education and medical services is lower, but the pressure in price rise and employment increases*

The cruising data in Table 1.5 shows that urban and rural residents thought the main pressure in life is the price rise; nearly 80% of interviewees said that their family living standard has been influenced by the price rise. The consumer price index (CPI) was precisely at a high level from May to September 2008; after September, the CPI fell and the price pressure was likely reduced.

In addition, urban and rural residents' bigger pressure in life is also manifested in "low household incomes and difficult daily life" (49.9%), "bad housing conditions and the inability to afford a house" (47.2%), as well as "family members are jobless, and dealing with unemployment or unstable jobs" (38.4%).

As compared with the first survey in 2006, the pressures in the medical service and education have been alleviated to an extent. The proportion of families that faced "high expenses in medical service that were difficult to bear" and "high educational expenses for children that were difficult to bear" had, respectively, dropped from 45.5% and 34% to 36.9% and 26.8%, which may be attributed to the coverage expansion of medical insurance for urban and rural residents to a certain extent in the two years prior to the survey, as well as the execution of compulsory education policy. But urban and rural residents' pressure in work and employment actually increased steadily, and the proportion of families under this pressure rose from 30% in 2006 to 38.4% in 2008.

When one has security in occupation and income, one can more easily deal with the pressures of life. Through the further survey of urban and rural residents' employment status, we discovered that it was not optimistic. It is calculated that the unemployment rate of those surveyed reached as high as 9.4%.[4] Comparatively, central and western urban

---

[4]Urban unemployment rate = the urban unemployed/(the urban unemployed + the urban employed) × 100%.

Table 1.5.   Urban and Rural Families' Pressure in Life (in 2006, in 2008).

	In 2008 Sample size = 7,139	In 2006 Sample size = 7,061
Rise in prices, influences living standard	79.91	—
Lower household income, daily life is with difficulty	49.98	51.31
Bad housing conditions, cannot afford house	47.17	45.01
Family members are jobless, dealing with unemployment or unstable job	38.43	30.06
High expenses in medical service that were difficult to bear	36.91	45.51
Many expenses in human relationship that were difficult to bear	32	34.82
Social convention goes bad, worry to be swindled and family is affected by it	27.13	23.31
High educational expenses for children that were difficult to bear	26.77	34
Public order goes bad, often fear	25.09	24.47
Overcharge in supporting the elder	18.77	22.33

Note: Unit: %.

unemployment rates were more distinct. The urban unemployment rate in large or medium-sized cities was higher than small cities (see Table 1.6). The majority of these urban unemployed populations (80% above) were non-agricultural labor, and 85% were 18- to 49-year-old young adults. Of this percentage, nearly 30% of people were newly unemployed who had lost their jobs in the previous year.

C. *Social security system covering urban and rural areas was just established, but the status of labor and social security in non–state-owned economic organizations needs urgent improvement*

The coverage of social security for urban and rural residents has been expanded. The cruising data in Table 1.7 indicate that, for 18- to 69-year-old non-agricultural population, urban endowment insurance (which contains

Li Peilin and Li Wei

Table 1.6.   Unemployment Rate Surveyed in Economically Active Populations.

	Unemployment rate surveyed (%)	Base number (person)
Urban economically active populations	**9.4**	**2,288**
East	7.5	992
Central	10.4	794
West	11.7	502
Large and medium-sized cities	10.1	1,210
Small cities	8.7	1,078

Table 1.7.   Urban and Rural Residents' Participation Rate in Social Security.

	Participated	Not participate	Do not know	Sample size
Urban endowment insurance	52.7	46.7	0.7	2,750
Rural endowment insurance	5.7	93.5	0.8	4,381
Urban medical insurance	58.7	40.5	0.8	2,750
New rural cooperative medical service	83.8	15.4	0.8	4,384
Unemployment insurance	20.7	77.9	1.3	2,748
Workers' compensation insurance	16.2	82.1	1.7	2,747

Note: (1) The urban endowment insurance includes the basic endowment insurance for urban residents and the enterprise's supplemental endowment insurance; urban medical insurance includes basic medical insurance for urban employees and medical insurance for urban residents. (2) The participation rate of urban endowment insurance, urban medical insurance, unemployment insurance, and workers' compensation insurance was counted by non-agricultural population; the participation rate of rural endowment insurance and the new rural cooperative medical system was counted by the agricultural population. Unit: %.

the basic endowment insurance for urban residents and the enterprise's supplemental endowment insurance) has nearly 53% coverage, and urban medical insurance (contains the basic medical insurance for urban employees and the medical insurance for urban residents) has approximately 58.7% coverage.

The proportion of insured persons through unemployment insurance and workers' compensation insurance is lower, at 20% and 16.2%, respectively. For agricultural residents in the same age group, 83.8% participated in the "new rural cooperative medical system", but rural social endowment insurance has 5.7% coverage because it was only carried out in a short time.

The participation rate of social security has something to do with the employment unit. The data in Table 1.8 shows that, in urban population, people worked in public enterprises and the cooperative ventures, and solely foreign-funded enterprises have higher participation proportions in all kinds of social security. For instance, in Party and government organizations, state-owned/collective enterprises, state-owned/collective

Table 1.8. Participation Rate of Social Security in Different Types of Enterprises.

	Sample size	Urban endowment insurance	Urban medical insurance	Unemployment insurance	Workers' compensation insurance
Party and government organizations, mass organization	73	67.7	88.6	23.6	27
State-owned and state-owned holding enterprises	262	87.2	84	62.5	52.6
State-owned/ collective institutions	301	79.3	87.4	47.6	32.2
Collective enterprises	45	84.1	86.9	55.9	53.2
Cooperative ventures and solely foreign-funded enterprises	71	88.4	74.1	72.1	67.2
Private enterprise	376	58.3	58.2	24.2	22.1
Individual units of industry and commerce	326	29.1	35.4	2.8	2.9

Note: Unit: %.

institutions, and cooperative ventures and solely foreign-funded enterprises, the coverage of urban endowment insurance is 67% to 88%, but
the proportion in private enterprises is only 58.3%, while less than 30%
of employees who worked in individual units of industry and commerce
participated in urban endowment insurance.

Except for social security, in terms of labor rights and interests security, there is a big difference in different types of enterprises. Table 1.9
shows the signing situation of employees' labor contracts in different
types of enterprises. It is observed that there is a high signing rate of

Table 1.9.   Signing Status of Labor Contract in Different Types of Enterprises.

				Distribution of signing mode		
	Sample number	Proportion of not signing labor contract	Proportion of signing labor contract	Continue contract before 2008	Renew contract in January 2008	Start to sign contract in January 2008
State-owned and state-owned holding enterprises	294	14.1	80.1	57.2	17.2	5.7
Collective enterprise	78	38.9	57.9	37.9	16.1	4
Cooperative ventures and solely foreign-funded enterprises	133	9.8	80.5	31.1	40.4	8.9
Private enterprise	813	52.5	41.3	20.6	14.4	6.3
Individual units of industry and commerce	150	87.7	11.3	2.4	6.2	2.7

Note: Unit: %.

labor contracts in state-owned enterprises and cooperative ventures and solely foreign-funded enterprises and, respectively, 80.1% and 80.5% of employees signed labor contracts; there was lower signing rates among collective enterprises at 57.9%, 16% lower in private enterprise, at 41.3%; and only 11.3% of employees signed contracts in individual units of industry and commerce. It is worth noting that all types of enterprises corrected and signed the labor contracts in January 2008 when the "Law of Labor Contracts" came into force. These were mainly cooperative ventures and solely foreign-funded enterprises, and 40.4% renewed their contracts. This reflected the tendency that enterprises dodged undertaking obligations for workers' security of rights and interests. The improvement of employed people's labor and social security status should be paid attention to in non-state-owned economic organizations, in private enterprise, and in individual units of industry and commerce from now on.

II. Public Opinions on Social Problem and Social Contradiction

A. *Rising prices, medical service, income differentials, and unemployment are the most distinct social problems*

In 18 social problems given in the survey (see Table 1.10), the top three items were thought to be "rise in prices" (63.5%), "difficulty and expense of seeing a doctor" (42.1%), and "oversized income differential" (28%). From fourth to seventh were, respectively, "employment and unemployment" (26%), "excessively high housing price" (20.4%), "embezzlement and corruption" (19.4%), as well as "retirement safeguards" (17.7%). From eighth to tenth were, respectively, "environmental pollution" (11.8%), "charging in education" (11.4%), and "social order" (9%). Except for "rise in prices", all these belonged to the transient problems of the year, ordering of other social problems is not obviously different than the first survey result in 2006.

Because of different interests, urban and rural residents have different respective social problems. As compared with rural population, urban residents thought that "employment and unemployment" and "excessively

Table 1.10.   Comprehensive Ordering of Social Problem.

		Urban and rural areas		Region		
	Whole	Urban area	Rural area	East	Central	West
Rise in prices	**63.5**	62.9	64	63.3	64.7	61.7
Being difficult and expensive to see a doctor	**42.1**	39.1	44.8	40.2	41.6	46
Oversized income differential, popularization between the rich and poor	**28**	28.2	27.8	26.2	27.6	31.6
Employment and unemployment	**26**	34.4	18.3	25	25.9	28
Excessively high housing price	**20.4**	30.5	11	25.4	17.1	17.7
Embezzlement and corruption	**19.4**	20.8	18.1	19.9	19.2	18.9
Retirement safeguard	**17.7**	17.5	18	14.3	21.5	17
Environmental pollution	**11.8**	12.7	11	17	9.1	8.1
Charging in education	**11.4**	11.2	11.6	10.9	12.5	10.5
Social order	**9**	9.2	8.9	11.2	7.7	7.8
Gap between urban and rural areas	**8**	3.9	11.9	7.1	8.7	8.3
Social convention	**7.4**	7.8	7.2	8.4	7.8	5.4
Sample size	**7,135**	3,424	3,711	2,677	2,786	1,672

Note: Unit: %.

high housing prices" were more relative to their vital interests, 34.4% and 30.5% urban residents put them on top three social problems, and so did only 18.3% and 11% rural residents, respectively. On the contrary, in rural residents' opinions, "difficulty and expense of seeing a doctor" was a social problem (44.8%) that needed to be solved urgently, while urban residents who held this view dropped 5%. Rural residents thought that "gap between urban and rural areas" was a main social problem, which was also greatly more than urban residents (11.9%:3.9%)

In the regional differential, the east's public paid more attention to "housing prices", "environmental pollution", and "social order" than central and western regions. Central regions' residents thought that "old age support" was a serious social problem. Western regions' residents thought that "difficulty and expense to see a doctor" and "oversized income differential" were more serious problems.

B. *Most have realized the conflict of interests among social groups, but 39% feel that the contradiction would not be intensified*

In the survey, we investigated the public's awareness of the conflicts of interest among social groups. The results indicated that only 17.1% people thought China was "without conflict", 45.1% thought there was "a little conflict", 15.7% thought there were "many conflicts", 4.7% thought there was a "serious conflict", and the other 17.1% felt it was "hard to tell". This result indicated that, on one hand, the overwhelming majority of urban and rural residents affirmed social harmony and stability as a whole, but on the other hand, 22.2% of people thought there were serious conflicts of interest between social groups.

We investigated the public's future judgment to the conflict of interest among social groups by this question: "Has the contradiction between social groups become intensified?" The results indicated that 38.6% people thought the contradiction would not be intensified (i.e., thought "would not be intensified absolutely" or "unlikely to be intensified"), 36.3% had the opposite judgment and thought that the contradiction will be possibly intensified (i.e., thought "will be intensified absolutely" or "possible to be intensified"), and 25.1% hesitated and thought it was hard to tell whether the contradiction would be intensified or not (see Table 1.11). As compared with the result of the first survey in 2006, the proportion of urban and rural residents who held optimistic judgment to the present situation of the conflicts of interest and development trends slightly rose, and the proportion that held a pessimistic manner slightly dropped, but the proportion of "hard to tell" also went up.

Table 1.11. Distribution of the Cognition on Conflict of Interest among Social Groups (in 2006, in 2008).

Question: whether to have the conflict of interest among social groups			Question: whether is the contradiction between social groups possibly intensified		
Answer option	In 2008	In 2006	Answer option	In 2008	In 2006
Serious conflict	4.7	4.8	Will be intensified absolutely	4.5	5
More conflicts	15.7	18.2	Possible to be intensified	31.8	33.6
A little conflict	45.1	44.9	Unlikely to be intensified	28.5	30.4
Without conflict	17.3	16.3	Would not be intensified absolutely	10.1	8.6
Hard to tell	17.1	15.8	Hard to tell	25.1	22.4
Sample number	7,139	7,061	Sample number	7,139	7,061

Note: Unit: %.

C. Currently the conflict of interest among social groups mainly focuses on the contradiction between the rich and the poor and the conflict between the cadres and masses

The public's views on the conflict of interest among social groups mainly focuses on a series of judgments regarding the difference and conflict among social groups. In the survey, we listed seven pairs of social groups with corresponding relations to ask "which two groups have the biggest difference" and "which two groups are easiest to have contradiction". The results indicated that, whether from the angle of difference or from the angle of easiness in having the conflict, "the poor and the rich" and "cadres and masses" were the top two options (see Table 1.12). This indicated that the relations between the rich and the poor and between the cadres and the masses are the social interest relations which at present urgently need attention. It is noteworthy that, because of the relations between administrating and being administrated, "employer and employee" and "supervisor and supervisee" also were regarded as potential sources of conflicts in interest.

Urban and rural residents' judgments regarding the beneficiary group also have similar distributions. When asking "which groups have obtained

Table 1.12. Urban and Rural Residents' Judgments to the Probability on the Difference and Conflict Among Social Groups.

Social groups	Which two groups have the biggest difference	Which two groups are easiest to have the contradiction
Poor and the rich	56.5	24.7
Cadres and masses	16.1	23.6
Urban and rural residents	7.8	5.7
Manual workers and brain workers	6.5	3.4
High and low education levels	4.1	2.3
Employer and employee	2.9	17.8
Supervisor and supervisee	2.4	12.9
Hard to tell	3.6	9.8
Sample size	7,139	7,139

Note: Unit: %.

the most benefits in the past 10 years", the top three groups were officials (68.8%), operator of state-owned/collective enterprises (60.4%), and bosses of private enterprises (52.3%). Moreover, the bottom three groups are migrant laborers (6.7%), workers (6.8%), and farmers (16%). This reflected the importance to handle the relations between cadres and masses carefully (see Figure 1.2).

III. Urban and Rural Residents' Sense of Security, Sense of Justice, and Degree of Satisfaction

A. *There is a higher sense of security as a whole, but food and traffic safety are concerns*

In the survey, the sense of security of the individual and family property, personal information and privacy, traffic, work, medical services, and food was inquired about; we discovered that 74.6% people thought they were "very safe" or "safer". Among them the highest scores is in personal sense of safety ("very safe" and "safer" total up 83.2%), but the lowest scores were in the food and traffic safety, which, respectively, were at only 65.3% and 65.7% (see Table 1.13), with over 30% of the respondents thinking these two categories were "unsafe". It is worth mentioning that in both

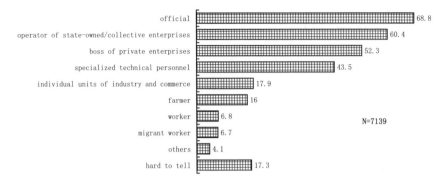

Figure 1.2. Distribution of Urban and Rural Residents' Judgments Regarding Beneficiary Group (%).

Table 1.13. Urban and Rural Residents' Sense of Security.

	Whole	Urban area	Rural area
Personal safety	83.2	81.4	85
Safety of individual and the family property	80.1	77.6	82.4
Labor safety	78.6	76.5	80.4
Safety of personal information and privacy	77.2	71.4	82.4
Medical safety	72.5	68.3	76.3
Traffic safety	65.3	63	67.4
Food safety	65.7	60.9	70.2
Sample size	7,139	3,426	3,713

Note: Unit: %.

2006 and 2008 surveys, food safety was a main concern. This worry was fully verified by the milk powder scandal in 2008.[5]

In urban and rural areas, rural residents have a greater sense of security in various aspects. Among them, a big differential is in the safety of personal information and privacy; 82.4% of rural residents thought it was "safe", but for urban residents, the answer was lower by 11%. In terms of food safety, 26.7% and 40% of rural and urban residents, respectively, thought food was "unsafe".

---

[5]Our survey started from June 2008, and finished in September 2008; therefore, the most of answers to "food safety" in the survey was not influenced by the reports about the event of "Sanlu powdered milk" at least.

B. Sense of justice in compulsory education and public medical service has been greatly enhanced, but fell obviously in the income differential

The survey indicated that urban and rural residents held an affirmative attitude to the current degree of social justice as a whole. A total of 68.4% people gave the appraisal of "very fair" or "fairer" to the entire Chinese society, which was 6% higher than the first survey in 2006. The sense of social justice was higher than 50% regarding the compulsory education system (85.77%), the college entrance examination system (74.44%), public medical services (66.77%), political rights (65.43%), the judicial and the law enforcement systems (52.85%), and the social security system, including endowment insurance (50.19%). Among them, the sense of fairness in compulsory education, public medical service, and social security system raised 9% to 15%, since 2006. This rise in approval fully reflected the government's job performance in these fields (see Table 1.14).

The sense of justice was lower than 50% in selecting party and government officials (47.22%), labor and employment opportunities (41.05%), the treatment between urban and rural areas (40.37%), the development between different areas (37.7%), the treatment between industries (35.24%), and income differentials (28.58%). Among them, the sense of justice in the income differential dropped 11% over that of 2006. The sense of justice regarding labor and employment opportunities also slightly dropped over the findings in 2006, which also reflected the increase of employment pressure and the aforementioned severe urban employment situation.

C. About 60% of urban and rural residents are basically satisfied with local government's work, but have more expectation for environmental protection and punishing embezzlement and corruption

Urban and rural residents' appraisal of local government's work in 11 aspects indicated that the public's average satisfaction rate was close to 60% (59.75%). Among them, the satisfaction rate in the compulsory education, the health services, and the maintenance of social order was more than 70%; the satisfaction rate in social security, economic development, information

Table 1.14.   Public's Sense of Justice to Different Social Domains (in 2006, in 2008).

Social fairness domains	Findings in 2008	Findings in 2006	Social fairness domains	Findings in 2008	Findings in 2006
Compulsory education	85.77	76.73	Labor and employment opportunity	41.05	44.45
College entrance examination system	74.44	71.44	Treatment between the urban and rural areas	40.37	28.97
Public medical service	66.77	49.86	Development between different areas	37.70	33.60
Enjoying the political right	65.43	61.95	Treatment between industries	35.24	33.60
Judicature and the law enforcement	52.85	55.12	Income differential	28.58	40.21
Social security including the endowment insurance etc.	50.19	37.51	Social fairness as a whole	68.35	62.27
Selecting the party and government officials	47.22	34.44	**Sample size**	**7,139**	**7,161**

Note: Unit: %.

disclosure, environmental protection, handling affairs according to the law, and increasing employment ranged from 50% to 62% (see Table 1.15). The low degree of satisfaction of urban and rural residents to local government's work was mostly in housing, namely in "providing low-rent housing and affordable housing", and the top two were "being honest and upright in performing their duties and punishing corruption", which indicated that work in this aspect was also highly expected. In addition, employment boosts, fair law enforcement, and environmental protection also had low degree of satisfaction. It is worth noting that this low degree of satisfaction to the government's

Table 1.15. Public's Degree of Satisfaction in Local Government's Work.

	Satisfaction rate	Dissatisfaction rate	Don't know
Providing high-quality basic education	78.52	15.66	5.82
Providing good medical service	71.16	24.81	4.03
Cracking down on crime and maintaining social order	70.15	26.26	3.59
Providing widespread social security	61.69	31.36	6.95
Developing economy and increasing income	60.68	32.36	6.96
Information disclosure and enhancing transparency of government's work	57.12	27.90	14.98
Protecting environment and treating pollution	56.53	39	4.47
Handling affairs according to law, fair law enforcement	56.49	33.52	9.99
Job enlargement and increasing employment opportunity	53.75	32.93	13.32
Be honest and upright in performing their duties and punishing corruption	48.11	38.79	13.10
Providing low-rent housing and affordable housing	43.01	31.13	25.85
Average	59.75	30.34	9.91

Note: In this table, satisfaction rate = very satisfied + percentage of more satisfied; Dissatisfaction rate = very dissatisfied + percentage of few satisfied; Satisfaction rate + dissatisfaction rate + do not know = 100%. Unit: %.

work was also in those domains where a high proportion of urban and rural residents "did not know", which indicated that, in order to enhance urban and rural residents' degree of satisfaction to the government's work, it is necessary to further enhance information transparency and to assure that people are made aware of programs. It should be pointed out that, from the angle of dissatisfaction rate, the local government's work was given the worst appraisal in environmental protection, nearly 40% of urban and rural residents were dissatisfied with it. In recent years, the social conflict caused by environmental problems has increased notably; more attention should be given to environmental protection.

IV. Countermeasures and Suggestions on Improving People's Livelihoods

A. *Increasing employment promotion and assistance strength*

Employment is the foundation of peoples' livelihood. In the survey, difficulty obtaining employment and unstable jobs were the main pressures in life. Positive employment policy should be unceasingly implemented, and aid to entrepreneurs in funds, products, skill training, and tax revenue should be strengthened to reduce the threshold of establishing businesses; training programs for labor should be strengthened; the education system should deal with the changes in the employment market of the future, vocational education should be positively developed, and diverse employment services should be provided for graduates.

B. *Consummating collective services such as medical services, education, housing, and social security*

In the survey results, urban and rural residents were satisfied with policies regarding medical services, education, and social security implemented in recent years. There is still much work to be done to establish the social security system covering urban and rural areas. From now on, the key point of social security is to further expand urban and rural coverage of medical insurance and endowment insurance so that more families have the ability to pay for healthcare. It is also important to further enhance the overall planning range of social security, and to formulate a national unified transfer and continuation of social security. In a related matter, it is important to consummate a housing safeguard system and provide low-rent and affordable housing.

C. *Strengthening monitoring and supervision of social risks*

The high frequency of food safety incidents has poorly influenced the Chinese economy and even the "Made in China" label; simultaneously, it has also exposed the shortage of supervision in product safety that has been so for a long time. Not only should good investments and a management environment be created for the enterprises, but industrial supervision functions should be strengthened also. How to deal with various social risks should be pondered over emphatically under the background of economic globalization, market integration, industrial chain, and popularization of products.

D. *Severely clamping down on embezzlement and corruption, strengthening the checks and balances of power, and establishing fair reasonable income distribution mechanisms*

Some unjust social phenomena have been denounced for a long time. This is mainly because of the power and money transactions caused by the shortage of checks and balances of power. China needs a system in place for the prevention of corruption; a system for registration and declaration of personal income and property should be positively explored and established, and property review mechanisms are needed. Fair reasonable income distribution mechanisms should be established, and the urban and rural dualistic structure should be gradually eradicated to reverse the tendency of income differential expansion. Policymakers should also attempt to eliminate the influence of unreasonable illegal factors in income distribution. The construction of an honest diligent government should be strengthened, and the relations between cadre and masses should be tended to in order to promote social justice by highly effective, friendly, honest and upright, open government ruling.

Chapter 2

China in the Mass Consumption Stage

Tian Feng

More than a decade ago, it was a status symbol for a family to have a house, a car, a mobile phone, and a computer; however, by the mid-2000s, these goods had become common people's "durable goods in daily life". Since then, televisions, refrigerators, and washing machines have entered most households. China's per capita gross domestic product (GDP) entered the rank of medium low-income countries, urban and rural residents' Engel's coefficient fell to about 34%, and housing and cars became widely available. This transformation symbolized China's entry to an economy of mass consumption.

China joined the World Trade Organization (WTO) in 2003 and entered a new round of growth in which GDP growth rate was at 10% or higher. The country depended on the drive of investment and import-export trade, and the dependency on foreign trade (the proportion of import-export trade in GDP) accounted for up to 70% of total economy; fluctuating risk was also hidden in it. The 2008 global financial crisis greatly influenced China's import-export trade; the economic growth subsided; and a series of economic and social consequence was brought about. China realized that it must transform the development path and must massively stimulate and develop the domestic demand so that China's future long-term growth can be less dependent on foreign markets.

I. Urban and Rural Residents' Consumption Patterns and Characteristics

A. Consumption levels continuously rise and China enters a stage of mass consumption as a whole

Chinese people's consumption level has continuously increased in recent times. As compared with the results of the CSS 2006, in the 2008 survey, gross consumer expenditures rose from RMB 17,388 to RMB 22,555, the consumption pattern also further improved, and as a symbol of family living standards, the Engel's coefficient (the proportion of family food expenditure in gross consumer expenditures) further dropped from 36.6% in 2006 to 34% in 2008. In 2008, in terms of urban and rural household consumer expenditures, the top three consumption types were food, education, and medical services, which respectively, accounted for 34%, 11.5%, and 10.6% of total expenditures. China's consumption pattern has completed a transition from survival to a stage of mass consumption.

Generally speaking, in urban and rural household consumer expenditures, the proportion of survival consumption (including food and clothing) is approximately 40.9% of total expenditures, and the proportion of development consumption (including housing, traffic, communication, culture and education, entertainment, healthcare, and traveling) occupied over 50% of total expenditures. Consumer expenditures have greatly surpassed those of the survival, and China's consumption pattern has completed the transition from that of survival to development.

According to the 2008 survey, the proportion of expenditures in education and medical services in total expenditures of urban and rural household consumption was quite high, respectively, accounting for 11.5% and 10.6%; in the 2006 survey, the result was close to this, but at that time, the proportion of medical expenditures was slightly higher than education. The high proportion of household consumer expenditure in education and medical services showed the development trend of household consumption patterns' upgrading, namely after having enough food and clothing. The human capital investment in education and health is being taken quite seriously — not only for enjoyment of life. The survey also indicated that expenditures in education and medical service, relative to urban and rural residents' income levels at present, were still very high. The financial burden in education and medical services has become a prominent issue, affecting the improvement of residents' general quality of life. The educational system's transformation and medical system reform in China will regard reducing the common families' burden in education and medical services as the priority target.

In addition, China's social expenditures accounted for a big proportion of total consumption, and on average reached 7.6%, which was the fourth largest expenditure (see Figure 2.1). Paying great attention to interpersonal relations is a characteristic of China's social life, but excessively high social expenditures can affect household consumption. The survey results showed that the proportion of rural family's social expenditures was higher than those of urban families, which also illustrated the characteristic that social expenditure was higher in tightly knit communities. Through the expansion of rural institutional community service, social conventions should be transformed gradually, thus, enhancing better spending habits.

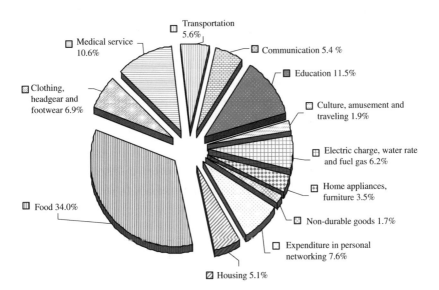

Figure 2.1. Urban and Rural Families' Consumption Pattern.

B. Degree of commercialization for urban and rural resident consumption is high, but consumption characteristics have different levels of stratification

In terms of expenses in commodities and services, urban and rural residents' stratification of consumption has improved. In the choice of clothes, the proportion of urban and rural populations that chose to make clothes themselves was very low: 0.6% in city and 0.8% in countryside. This indicated that the overwhelming majority of residents have become accustomed to buying commodities and services, and clothing has become a kind of consumer product that is widely purchased. Ordinary families' purchase of commodities and services has caused clothing commercialization, which indicated that urban and rural residents have become relatively more developed consumer group.

In terms of purchasing clothes, urban populations take the quality and brand of clothes quite seriously; over 50% of people purchase clothes in big stores and specialty shops, thus, indicating that the urban proportion was much higher than the rural proportion. Rural population regards clothes as non-durable consumables; most buy their clothes at rural markets, while some purchase clothing at ordinary shops and from street peddlers.

Dining out has also become urban and rural residents' regular choice: over 40% of rural populations dined out frequently, and the proportion of urban population was higher, at 56.6%. Rural population dined out mainly in snack bars and small food shops. The choice of urban populations was relatively various and balanced; general restaurants and mid-grade restaurant were often chosen.

C. Household consumption level assumes a terraced distribution, and high-income households have increased

According to the principles of dividing income levels into five parts, urban and rural families were respectively divided into five economic types by household income level, namely the lower, lower-middle, middle, upper-middle, and upper-income levels. Through analysis, we discovered that, whether in city or in countryside, a range from lower-income families to high-income families all appeared. The household consumption level assumed a step distribution, namely the high-income families had higher consumption levels. All income levels experienced a growth trend of consumption that was steady, but high-income household consumption levels rose suddenly. This also indicated the differential between the high consumption family and the general family in consumption level was also expanding.

In this survey, we discovered that high-income household consumption levels had a large differential in relation to the other income groups, the absolute amount of high-income household consumption was approximately equal to the sum of middle-income and upper-middle income households' combined. Taking the city as the example, a middle-income family's average consumer expenditure was RMB 24,790.5, while upper-middle-income households' average was RMB 31,508.7, and the sum of both was only RMB 526.6 more that high-income family levels of RMB 55,772.6 (see Figure 2.2).

D. *Durable consumer goods have a high diffusion rate, and rural consumption has huge development potential*

With the development of market economies and the increase of household income, the consumption pattern has upgraded steadily. Consumer durable goods have become more popular. Color TVs, mobile phones,

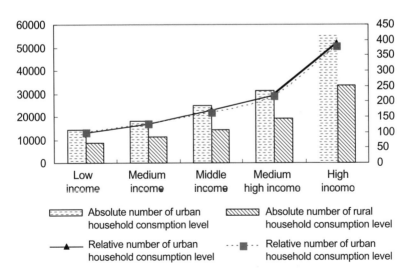

Figure 2.2. Urban and Rural Consumption Level Under Different Incomes.

refrigerators, washers, cars, and personal computers have become the new consumption hotspots.

Urban and rural families were similar in terms of their possession of consumer durable goods; the difference was small in the possession of color TVs and telephones, which have become popular among medium and low-income families. There were obvious differences in terms of the possession of refrigerators, washers, microwave ovens, and cameras because of different lifestyles in urban and rural areas. As emerging consumer durable goods, the possession of personal computers and cars in rural families was much lower than in urban families.

An important discovery in this survey is that the possession of cars, computers, and mobile phones in urban and rural families, even low-income families, was higher than anticipated. Household income was divided into five parts; every 100 urban high-income households had 27.5 cars, with 14.8 in rural households, whereas every 100 urban low-income families had 5.3 cars, with 2.4 in rural households; every 100 urban high-income households had 99 computers, with 26.8 in rural households, whereas every 100 urban low-income families also had 21.7 computers, with 3.1 in rural households. Every 100 urban high-income households had 259.5 mobile phones, with 235.5 in rural households, whereas every 100 urban low-income families had 115.4 mobile phones, with 75.3 in rural households. This indicated that emerging consumer durable goods are popular in all kinds of stratifications of consumption. There is still very big consumption potential at all income levels.

In terms of consumer desire, high-income families had the most intense purchasing desire for consumer durable goods; low-income families' purchasing desire was also slightly higher than medium low-income families', which possibly had something to do with low possession levels of consumer durable goods. In the bulk buying of consumer durable goods, high-income households were still the main consumer group.

Although the possession of consumer durable goods in rural families was lower than urban families, their purchasing desires were actually higher than urban families. Different stratifications of rural families' purchasing desire were higher than that of urban families. Low possession of consumer durable goods in rural markets and high purchasing desire is advantageous in enhancing the rural domestic demand and in driving economic growth. Presently, the implementation of the policy of "home appliances going to the countryside" gives subsidies for rural families to purchase home appliances, which is advantageous to activate farmers' purchasing power, to hasten the upgrading of rural consumption, to expand rural consumption, and to promote the harmonious development of domestic and external demands. The income and consumption levels of rural households were lower, however.

II. Differences and Problems in Urban and Rural Household Consumption

A. *Urban and rural household consumption levels and patterns are different*

The cruising data showed that the urban household consumption level is obviously higher than rural household consumption level. Urban household's average consumption amount is RMB 28,343.7, while it is RMB 17,285 in rural households. The three items with the biggest differentials are food, housing, and education; food expenses account for RMB 9,790.2 in urban areas, and RMB 5,751.0 in rural areas; housing expenses account for RMB 1,865.9 in urban areas, and RMB 484.7 in rural areas; education expenses account for RMB 3,170.5 in urban area, and RMB 2,069.2 in rural areas. There is also an obvious urban and rural differential in other consumption levels as well. In the survey results, except for the non-durable goods and social expenses, urban and rural household consumption was quite different.

In the current consumption pattern, urban and rural families did not have an obvious difference in basic survival expenditures; expenditures in food and clothing accounted for 41.4% and 40.1%, respectively, of total household consumer expenditures. Urban and rural families had obvious differences in development expenditure structure, especially in housing and medical services. Because of high house prices in urban areas in recent years, the proportion of consumer expenditure concerning housing increased obviously and occupied 6.6% of total expenditures, which was much higher than the 2.8% of rural housing expenditures. Although the rural medical insurance system basically covered all rural families in 2008, rural family's medical expenses accounted for 12.4% of total expenditures, which were higher by 3% than the 9.4% spent by urban families. The proportion of expenditures in education and human relationships was also higher than in urban families. In addition, the difference between urban and rural families' expenditures in culture, entertainment, and traveling, although the consumption level was low, was also obvious; urban families spent an average of RMB 717.8, which accounted for 2.5%, while rural families averaged RMB 180.3, which accounted for 1% of total expenses (see Table 2.1).

Table 2.1. Urban and Rural Household Consumption Level and Consumption Pattern.

Consumption pattern	Urban family		Rural family	
	Amount	Proportion	Amount	Proportion
Housing	1865.9	6.6	484.7	2.8
Food	9,790.2	34.5	5,751.0	33.3
Clothing	1,957.6	6.9	1,171.7	6.8
Medical service	2,670.9	9.4	2,141.6	12.4
Traffic	1,425.0	5.0	1,107.0	6.4
Communication	1,482.9	5.2	965.8	5.6
Education	3,170.5	11.2	2,069.2	12.0
Culture, entertainment and traveling	717.8	2.5	180.3	1.0
Electric charge and water rate etc.	1,935.3	6.8	926.9	5.4
Home appliances and furniture	1,010.7	3.6	567.3	3.3
Non-durable goods	467.7	1.7	313.7	1.8
Human relationship	1,849.1	6.5	1,605.7	9.3
Total	28,343.7	100	17,285.0	100

B. Consumption in education and medical services assumes rigid characteristics, and low-income family's life quality is influenced

Theoretically, Engel's coefficient is an important parameter to determine the living standards of a family. Generally speaking, the higher the proportion of food expenditures in total household consumer expenditures, the lower is the family living standard and vice versa. The survey actually discovered that low-income family's food expenditures were low, and simultaneously its proportion in total expenditure was also low. Urban low-income family's average food expenditures were RMB 4,898.8, and the proportion of their total expenditures was 34.2%, which was higher than the proportion of high-income households (31.3%), but was lower than the proportion of lower middle-income families (39.1%), middle-income families (35%), and high-income families (36.6%). The situation was similar in rural areas: the low-income family's average food expenditure accounted for 29.8% of total expenditures, which was lower than other types of families, but its food consumption level was only RMB 2,637.1, which was much lower than other types of families.

Through the data, we discovered that there is a special situation in which low-income family's Engel's coefficient was lower because urban and rural low-income families lived frugally to guarantee consumption in education and medical services. In other words, consumption in education and medical services is a kind of special consumption, and it does not display consumption flexibility along with changes in income levels, but has the characteristic of consumption rigidity. For instance, urban low-income families' education expenses were as much as middle-income families, but the consumption proportion was much higher; rural low-income families' medical expenses were as much as middle-income families, but the consumption proportion was likewise much higher than for other types of families. In addition, urban low-income family's housing expenditures were also high.

Generally, under the limited consumption capacity, low-income families should first reduce the amount and proportion of development consumption expenditures to guarantee a basic quality of life; therefore, usually the flexibility of development consumer expenditures should be higher than that of survival consumer expenditures. Because Chinese families pay great attention to the education for children, as well as preparation for medical expenses, Chinese low-income families opt to rely on pinching and saving to safeguard expenditures for education and medical expenses. Under such a limited consumption capacity, survival expenditures affects more families than they should. This trend illustrates that increasing education investment and medical security to reduce ordinary families' financial burden is helpful to stimulate consumption and expand the domestic demand.

C. Overall household consumption rates are somewhat low, and the consumption rate is marginal along with the increase of income

The household consumption rate refers to the ratio between household consumer expenditures and the family's disposable income and is also called the household consumption tendency. The consumption rate is used to express the target of household consumer behavior. Chinese households' consumption rate was lower than that of the developed countries and other developing countries at same level, and the immediate consumption rates were not high. This is related to Chinese family culture and consumer ideals; there is a long tradition of diligence and thrift management. The majority of Chinese families put a large proportion of earnings in savings. Chinese have long suppressed immediate consumption so that they can later deal with uncertainties in housing, medical services, and education. Presently, Chinese economic growth still excessively depends on fixed asset investment and import-export trade. In the long run, if the savings ratios are maintained, there will not be enough domestic demand to drive the economy.

According to the survey, the average consumption rate of Chinese families was about 76%, and the urban households' consumption rate was 77.6%, which was higher than the 74.1% for rural families, which indicated that urban families' immediate consumption tendency was slightly higher than that of rural families.

The survey result indicated that, whether in the city or in the countryside, the household consumption rate decreases successively along with an increase of income. Low-income households' consumption rates reached as high as 90%, which means the low-income family's annual income was almost totally spent in consumption. High-income households' consumption rates were quite low and urban and rural high-income households' consumption rates were 57.9% and 53.9%, respectively, which means that high-income households used roughly 40% of annual income in savings and accumulation (see Figure 2.3).

Viewing from the angle of which increases in income stimulate consumption, increasing low-income households' income is more effective than increasing high-income households' income to stimulate consumption. If low-income households' income is increased, it is more possible to realize purchasing power, which can be more effective in enhancing consumer expenditure levels. On the contrary, the increase of a high-income household's income will only increase their savings and not drive the growth of commodity and service consumption in the short term. Therefore, from the angle of stimulating consumption and expanding domestic demand, it is an efficient path to enhance the consumption level of medium- and low-income families, which have more of a propensity to consume. However, the key in raising medium- and low-income household consumption levels still relies on income distribution; the consumption capacity of low-income households, particularly rural low-income households, is low; and through the mechanisms of multiple distribution, the differentials between urban and rural household incomes and between consumption levels can be reduced, and low-income households' income enhanced. Moreover, rural household income is lower than that of urban households, and rural

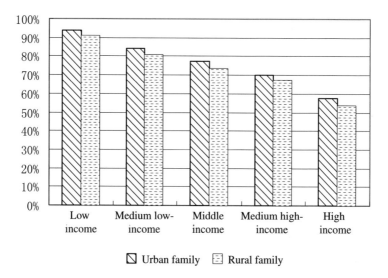

Figure 2.3. Ratio Between Urban and Rural Family Expenditure and Income Under Different Incomes.

household consumption rates are also lower than that of urban families. Therefore, by enhancing farmers' income, urban and rural dualistic structure is eradicated, and rural consumption is transformed.

III. Opinions and Suggestions on Promoting Consumption and Expanding Domestic Demand

Due to the financial crisis that initiated Chinese economic fluctuation and export shrinkage, promoting consumption, expanding domestic demand, and driving economic growth have become common priorities. Through the analysis of the CSS 2008 data, we see that people's livelihood should be emphatically invested in to promote consumption and to drive domestic demand, investment in employment, education, medical services, housing, and social security. The public fiscal system in these domains should be consummated and public products and services supply in these domains should be expanded to gradually eliminate the troubles they provide to consumer confidence.

A. *Developmental phase of household consumption, promoting consumption, guaranteeing growth, and employment*

Although the international financial crisis has had a profound influence on the Chinese economy, and the prospect of economic growth has been unstable, China has entered a stage of mass consumption as a whole. Urban and rural families are facing universal consumption upgrading; depending upon domestic demand to keep swift economic growth has had good foundations. Urban and rural families and residents have experienced rapid income growth, and consumption has risen accordingly. Therefore, the growth path must be transformed to drive economic growth that depends on domestic demand. The trend that the proportion of resident income and labor income in the national income distribution drops must be reversed thoroughly, and the proportion of resident income in national income distribution and the proportion of payment for labor in the primary channels of distribution should be gradually enhanced to strengthen the drive of resident consumption and ultimately economic growth.

B. *Improving housing, medical, and educational systems*

At present, China's social security system is not still perfect, and the swift growth of expenditures in education, medical services, and housing has disrupted the rhythm of normal consumption patterns. In household consumption, expenditures in education and medical services have strong rigidity, which not only has had a squeeze effect toward other expenditures to suppress normal household consumer expenditures but also has increased the household consumer expenditures for anticipated crisis. This has caused intense savings desire and low consumption rates. Ordinary family's savings strategy to deal with increases in education, medical service, and housing expenses is not favorable to stimulate consumption and expand domestic demand. Therefore, stimulating consumption and driving domestic demand must be established based on a series of relatively complete social security mechanisms, including housing, medical services, and education. Otherwise, it is difficult to form the complexion that enhances family and individual consumption wishes, and drives the growth of domestic demand.

C. *Consummating urban and rural equal public service systems and reducing the proportion of rural household consumer expenditures in public services*

As a result of the long-standing urban and rural dualistic structure, the rural public service system not only falls behind urban ones historically but also lacks the capacity to adapt to current social and economic development and has seriously influenced the rural families' quality of life and consumption levels. In particular, some public services cannot be enjoyed by rural families; through the survey, we discovered that the proportion of rural household consumer expenditures was higher than urban families in the public service domains, including medical service, education, and transportation. Obviously, rural household consumer expenditures in purchasing public services has become one of the substantial clauses for the difference between urban and rural consumption patterns, and the "reversal" between the consumption pattern and the consumption level. Therefore, rural public utilities should be swiftly developed and basic rural public service levels should be enhanced. Rural people's livelihoods should be improved emphatically according to the requirements that form new patterns of urban and rural economic and social development integration. The proportion of rural family's consumer expenditures in public services should be reduced to effectively avoid "reversal" between urban and rural consumption levels and structures, thus, reasonably driving rural households' consumption.

D. *Straightening out the relations of income distribution, emphatically helping rural and low-income families to increase the income*

Unreasonable relations of income distribution have widened the income differential as well as the consumption differential between different types of families and crowds. Because the high-income households' consumption rate is basically fixed, rural and low-income families' marginal propensity to consume is high, but the actual purchasing power is limited so that the whole social consumption capacity drops. In the survey, we discovered that although rural families' consumer desire for durable goods was higher than the city, rural consumption was in a relatively downturned condition because of limited income and low social security levels. This indicated that although government subsidies had stimulated rural household consumption, the consumption capacity of this group was still limited. Therefore, speaking of rural and low-income families, increasing income is the key to stimulate consumption. Especially in 2009, economic fluctuation had bigger impacts on rural and low-income families. Therefore, emphatically helping rural and low-income families to increase their income and reduce the income differential is beneficial to increase overall social consumption capacity and the stability of economic growth.

Chapter 3

Characteristic and Change of Current Employment

Fan Lei

In recent years, because of rapid economic growth, China's employment situation has been relatively steady. However, since the second half of 2008, the obvious influence of the global financial crisis on China has resulted in worsening of the employment situation, with many small- and medium-sized enterprises conducting massive lay-offs. This situation has triggered a mass return of laborers to their native villages. Therefore, employment has become the current focal point in people's lives, and recent graduates are finding it difficult to obtain employment.

I. Basic Features of Urban and Rural Employment Status

Through 30 years of reform, old employment patterns that featured planned distribution, sole systems of ownership, and urban and rural isolation has vanished. A new employment pattern that features general adoption of market principles, multiple systems of ownership, and urban and rural movement has emerged. In this market reforming process, employment has been the key problem in social and economic development. The huge population base has led to the creation of surplus labor supply, while the unreasonable structure of labor force has also caused labor shortages (e.g., shortage of migrant laborers and skilled workers). The rapid economic development has created massive new employment posts, leading to an increase in labor force and resulting in the surplus rural labor seeking employment. China needs to develop labor-intensive enterprises to be advantageous in increasing employment opportunities. China also needs to transform the economic growth paths to develop technical and capital-intensive enterprises. In this complex and crucial employment situation, China's new employment pattern presents a series of new characteristics.

A. *Preliminary formation of employment system based on market principle*

Since the reform and opening up, through the transition of dual-system employment, China has finally established a reform direction of an employment system based on market principles; its basic objective is to cultivate and push labor market development with steady steps and establish a labor market based on market distribution.

The labor contract system has become the foundation of employment based on the market principle. As the first step to break through ridged employment systems under planned economy, the pilot work of a labor contract system started in 1980. In the 1990s, the reform of the labor contract system was fully pushed, which had gradually disintegrated the fixed worker system under the traditional employment system. In January 2008, the implementation of the "Law of Labor Contracts of the People's Republic of China" (中华人民共和国劳动合同法) (*zhong hua ren min gong he guo lao dong he tong fa*) meant that the labor contract system reform had changed from breaking through traditional employment systems and pushing toward the formation of a labor market, to recruiting and using a work force on the premise of normalizing general adoption of market principles, as well as safeguarding worker's legitimate rights and interests. Perhaps, this historical transformation symbolizes the preliminary formation of an employment system based on market principles in China.

The survey results showed that 84.1% of workers in state-owned enterprises and in state-owned holding enterprises signed labor contracts, so did 90.4% of workers in cooperative ventures and in solely foreign-funded

Table 3.1. Signing of Labor Contract in all Types of Enterprises.

	State-owned enterprises and state-owned holding enterprises		Collective enterprise		Private enterprise		Cooperative ventures and solely foreign-funded enterprises	
	Frequency	**Percentage**	**Frequency**	**Percentage**	**Frequency**	**Percentage**	**Frequency**	**Percentage**
Signed labor contract before January 2008, and continue to present day	157	58.1	30	36.6	136	20	33	35.1
Signed labor contract before, and renewal of contract after January 2008	52	19.3	15	18.3	94	13.8	36	38.3
Without labor contract before, but signed labor contract after January 2008	15	5.6	3	3.7	32	4.7	10	10.6
Working in this unit since 2008, signed labor contract	3	1.1	1	1.2	23	3.4	6	6.4
Without labor contract	41	15.2	31	37.8	390	57.4	9	9.6
Do not know	2	0.7	2	2.4	5	0.7	0	0
Total	270	100	82	100	680	100	94	100

enterprises, as well as 59.8% in collective enterprises, and 41.9% in private enterprises. Simultaneously we may also see that, because the "Law of Labor Contracts of the People's Republic of China" has created suitable standards for present short-term labor contracts, in the non-public ownership enterprises, a relatively high proportion of staffs signed the labor contract after January 2008 and so did 38.3% of staffs in the cooperative ventures and in solely foreign-funded enterprises (see Table 3.1).

One of basic characteristics of the employment system based on market principles is the unrestricted flow of labor in the employment market. This unhindered flow realizes the market's disposition of the labor force. For a long time, the urban labor force in China has basically settled down after being distributed to their work units by administrative means, rendering it very difficult for them to move based on personal choice. Since the reform, the unrestricted flow of labor has become an important basis in forming an employment system based on market principles. In the survey on urban population, those who started their first job in the 1970s had worked in an average of 1.91 work units, those who started their first job in the 1980s had worked in an average of 1.99 units, and those who started their first job in the 1990s had worked on an average of 2.01 units. Although this result cannot comprehensively describe China's overall status of labor movement since the founding of Modern China, we can see that there is an increasingly frequent movement of urban labor since the reform.

The promotion of labor market intermediaries to obtain employment has appeared. In an employment system based on market principles, the labor market intermediary plays an important role as the professional organization of labor resource distribution. It saves search costs and reduces the job-hunting risk in the labor employment process. Under the influence of the traditional Chinese characteristics of interpersonal interaction, a job-hunting pattern based on individual social networks still occupies the key position in the labor movement based on the market principles. In the survey, 66.7% of unemployed people sought a job through their relatives and friends; however, we also found that while 14.9% of people once sought a job through employment service organizations and 10.5% sought employment by attending job fairs, only 4.1% sought jobs by government and enterprise's placement.

B. *Flexibility of the labor market is strengthened, and non-regular employment becomes an important employment form*

As a consequence of China's surplus labor supply and the massive lay-offs of workers in state-owned enterprises going through reform, since the mid-1990s, encouraging flexible employment has been one of the Chinese government's important actions of positive employment policy. Flexible employment is different from traditional employment in labor relations; working time, payment for labor, and work location are all subject to changes. Therefore, the problem of non-regular employment produced by it has gradually been attended to. The International Labor Organization discussed the concept of "non-regular employment" in 2002; the "non-regular sector" has been divided into three types: mini enterprise, family enterprise, and independent service provider. Wu Yaowu (吳要武) and Cai Fang (蔡昉) defined nine types of non-regular workers according to the definition of the International Labor Organization on non-regular employment in 2006, unifying the particularity in the Chinese reforming process.[1] According to sampling data of the Ministry of Human Resources and Social Security of China on "urban employment and social security" of 66 cities in 2002, China's proportion of non-regular employment was 40.3–45.2%, and the number of non-regular workers was 65.5 to 75.1 million people.

In the CSS 2008 data, we referred to Wu Yaowu and Cai Fang's classification standards to divide the employed population, and the result indicated that, among the interviewees, the non-regular employed population accounted for 49.8% of all non-agricultural labor. Thus, it can be seen that non-regular employment has become an important employment form in non-agricultural sector, and labor relations has become accordingly complicated (see Table 3.2).

According to the survey results, among the interviewees, non-regular workers were primarily middle-aged and old people with an education level of junior middle school and below; the lower the education level, the

---

[1] Wu Yaowu (吳要武) and Cai Fang (蔡昉) (2006) China's urban non-regular employment: Scale and feature. *China Labor Economics*, Vol. 3, pp. 69–70. Beijing: China Labor and Social Security Publishing House (CLSSPH).

Table 3.2. Composition of Non-regular Employed Population.

	Frequency	Percentage
Be employed, non-regular employee, without regular labor contract	413	33.9
Home part-time worker	20	1.6
Community post for public welfare	26	2.1
Home helper and the self-employed	468	38.4
Be employed, worker in individual economy	134	11
Non-regular employee in regular section	159	13
Total	1220	100

higher the non-regular employment proportion. In this group, the proportion of non-regular employment was above 60%. In the group comprising workers who attended technical college or pursued higher education, the proportion of regular employment[2] was more than 78%. In terms of age, the proportion of non-regular employment for people aged 39 years or younger was about 40–45%, about 50–60% for those aged between 40 and 59 years, and 77% for those aged 60 years and above. As a whole, in the non-regular employed population, people aged 35 years and above accounted for 73.93%. In the household registry, nearly two-third of non-agricultural workers in rural households were non-regular employees, but the proportion of non-regular employees in the urban household registry was 40.4%, which indicated that rural laborers were mainly non-regular employees in non-agricultural employment.

C. Non-agricultural employment has become rural residents' important employment source

Since the reform and opening up, with China's fast development of industrialization and urbanization, as well as the gradual relaxation of policy regarding population movement, the supply system of urban food, and the

---

[2]Regular employment includes regular employees in urban and rural state-owned and non-state-owned enterprises, or non-agricultural workers who sign the labor contract.

change of employment systems, large numbers of rural surplus labor left their lives as farmers; they either worked in local rural enterprises by the way of "leaving the land but not the countryside" or worked or did business in the city to form new labor troops — migrant laborer group that have a huge scale and huge function in China's social and economic development since the 1980s. The total population of this group reached 200 million people by 2004. They have become an important strength in China's industrialization and urbanization development.

Rural laborers' non-agricultural employment has loosened the former employment system of urban and rural isolation to a certain extent. Based on the survey results, in rural families, members of 63.8% of rural families have at least once had non-agricultural employment experiences, and at present, 55.7% of families still have some members engaged in non-agricultural occupations. In terms of individuals, 43.25% of people have had non-agricultural employment experience, of which one-fourth have presently returned to their native villages to work at farms after being engaged in non-agricultural occupations, and at present, 26.41% of rural population are still engaged in non-agricultural occupations. This means that in total, of the 700 million rural Chinese people, 300 million possessed non-agricultural employment experience, and nearly 80 million have returned to their village to work a farming post.

Since the reform, the rural population's non-agricultural employment experience has been classified into three different groups: the non-agricultural employment group, the group that returned to their native villages to work, and the farmer group without non-agricultural employment experience. They have obvious differences in terms of personal features.

In the group that had returned to their native villages to work farming jobs after working in the non-agricultural sector, men accounted for 63.7%; their average age was 43.2 years, and 56.9% were between 35 and 54 years; the education level was primarily junior middle school, and 9.6% possessed education at high school level or above. Women primarily accounted for the farmer group without non-agricultural employment experience: the proportion was 62.2%, the average age was 48.27 years, and 62.7% were aged between 40 and 59 years, the education level was primarily the elementary school level and below, and only 4% had reached high school and above. This indicated that the gender and the education level were major factors in affecting early rural residents' non-agricultural employment. In the non-agricultural employment group, men accounted for 55.4%, the average age was 38.7 years, 70.2% were atleast 44 years old, their education level was primarily junior middle school, and 22% completed high school and above. At present, in non-agricultural employment groups, the reduction in gender gap indicated that the number of women possessing non-agricultural employment experience have increased along with the increase in the education levels of women in recent years.

II. Issues on Urban and Rural Employment

In the process of formation and growth of China's labor market, the migrant labor's flexible employment, unemployed people's re-employment, and graduates' employment, as well as non-regular employment all have composed distinct collective issues with regard to China's employment situation.

A. *Unemployment on the rise*

After reform, because the educated youth often returned to the city, and the staff of state-owned enterprises were laid-off, large-scale unemployment existed in both groups. At present, with the preliminary establishment of an employment system based on market principles, the influence of domestic and foreign economic fluctuation on China's employment market is also becoming increasingly obvious.

In the past, China evaded the unemployment rate for a long time. In fact, until 1994, China only officially used the concept of "unemployment" and "urban registered unemployment rate". From the unemployment rate statistics announced, urban registered unemployed population at the end of the year, urban registered unemployment rates, or urban investigated unemployment rates were assumed to follow an upward trend since the 1990s. In 2000, the urban registered unemployed population at the end of the year was 8 million more than the previous year and the registered unemployment rate reached 4%; the investigated unemployment rate reached 8.12% after 2000, and approximately stabilized at 5–6% from

2001 to 2005. The cruising data in 2008 showed the urban-investigated unemployment rate to have reached 9.6% (see Figure 3.1).

In terms of the composition of urban unemployed population, people at the education level of junior middle school and below and the middle-aged crowd constitute the main unemployed group.

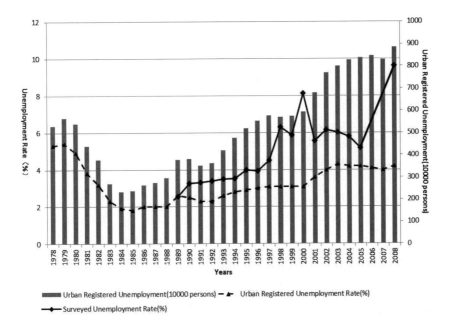

Figure 3.1. Urban Unemployed, Registered Unemployment Rate and Unemployment Rate of China Surveyed Since 1978.

Note: Because the abovementioned data of investigated unemployment rate is from different surveys, under the influence of respective scope of survey, sampling way, definition of concept and implementation of surveys etc., the investigated unemployment rate result is not comparable.

Data source: Urban registered unemployed population at the end of the year and registered unemployment rate are the data from *China Statistical Yearbook* (中国统计年鉴) (*zhong guo tong ji nian jian*) all previous years; investigated unemployment rate from 1989 to 1999 and from 2001 to 2004 was from P47 of *Reports On China's Population and Labor (2007)* (人口与劳动绿皮书（2007）) (*ren kou yu lao dong lü pi shu*) by Cai Fang as Chief Editor, Social Sciences Academic Press in 2007; the investigated unemployment rate in 2000 was calculated according to the data of national population census in 2000; the investigated unemployment rate in 2005 was calculated according to the data of the sampling survey of population of 1% in 2005; the investigated unemployment rate in 2008 was the cruising data of the CSS by the Institute of Sociology, the Chinese Academy of Social Sciences from May to August 2008, see Li Peilin and Chen Guangjin (2008); and urban registered unemployment rate in 2008 was the data of the fourth quarter of 2008 announced by the Ministry of Human Resources and Social Security.

In terms of urban unemployed population's education level, 15.9% reached elementary school or below, 40.1% reached junior middle school, 33% reached high school (including trade school, technical secondary school, and vocational senior middle school), and 11% reached junior college, which indicated that the unemployed population were mainly a product of a low education level, namely of junior middle school or below.

In terms of age structure among the urban unemployed population, 11.5% were aged 24 years and younger, 19.4% were aged between 25 and 34 years, 29.5% were aged between 35 and 44 years, 29.5% aged were between 45 and 54 years, and 10.1% were aged 55 years or older; this indicated that the unemployed population were mainly middle-aged people (35–54 years).

In the household register, whereas rural population accounted for 16.7%, urban population accounted for 83.3%, which indicated that the rural population that worked in cities accounted for a certain proportion in urban unemployment.

In terms of duration of unemployment, 21.3% of people lost their job less than a year earlier, 10.6% remained unemployed for over 1 year, 5.9% for over 2 years, 6.9% for over 3 years, 5.3% for over 4 years, and 50% for over 5 years. Generally speaking, long-term unemployment can hinder the unemployed worker's ability to obtain a job.

The urban unemployed have a lower degree of social security. At present, urban social security has big differences according to various employment types and respective professions. Du Yang (都阳) and Gao Wenshu (高文书) contrasted local labors' and migrant-workers' social security with the data of the "Survey of Floating Population Communities" by the Institute of Population and Labor Economics, the Chinese Academy of Social Sciences in 2003. Among them, the proportion that had endowment insurance was 77.35%, of which regularly employed people's coverage was 60–80%, while self-employed people were only covered 30% of the time; the proportion covered by medical insurance was 70.23%, of which 30.77% of small-businessmen and 35% of self-employed people were covered. The proportion of workers covered by unemployment insurance was 37.13%, and in private enterprises, it was only 4.35%. The proportion of workers covered by compensation insurance was 29.08%, and in the private enterprise, it was 13.04%. In terms of industries, the

Table 3.3. Urban Employed and Unemployed People's Social Security.

	Urban unemployed people		Urban employed people	
	Frequency	Percentage	Frequency	Percentage
Urban basic endowment insurance	62	27.3	902	41.7
Basic medical insurance for urban employees (including socialized medicine)	37	16.3	855	39.5
Unemployment insurance	10	4.4	511	23.6
Workers' compensation insurance	2	0.9	435	20.1
Urban and rural minimum living security	16	7	98	4.5

insured proportion of employed people in social service industry was lower than that of other industries (see Table 3.3).[3]

In this survey, urban employed people had lower coverage rates of social security, and urban unemployed people's coverage rates were lower than that of employed people. Only the insured rate of the unemployed population in urban minimum living security programs was slightly higher than the employed population and the coverage rate was much lower than that of urban employed people.

Familial pressures faced by the urban unemployed population are higher than that faced by the urban employed. The survey also indicated that families of the urban unemployed population face a higher proportion of life pressures than that of the urban employed population in the majority of areas, such as "rises in prices that influence living standards", "family members are jobless, unemployed or on an unstable job", and "lower household income causing difficulty". The latter two form more than 25% or higher than that of urban employed population.

[3] Du Yang (都阳) and Gao Wenshu (高文书) (2005). How far is China from unitary social security system [(中国离一元社会保障体系有多远) (*zhong guo li yi yuan she hui bao zhang ti xi you duo yuan*)]. *China Labor Economics*, Vol. 2, pp. 45–49. Beijing: China Labor and Social Security Publishing House (CLSSPH).

Table 3.4.   Life Pressures of Urban Employed and Unemployed Population's Families.

	Urban unemployed population (A)	Urban employed population (B)	(A–B)
Rise in prices, influences living standards	93.8	85.2	8.5
Family members unemployed or having unstable jobs	81.3	39.4	41.8
Lower household income, difficult daily life	72.8	45.2	27.5
Bad rented housing conditions, inability to afford own housing	58.9	49.2	9.8
High medical expenses	49.1	34.1	15.1
High educational expenses for children	37.9	31.2	6.7
Deterioration of social convention, worries about being swindled	36.6	31.2	5.5
Fear of deterioration of public order	34.4	28.9	5.5
Difficulty in bearing family expenses	31.7	31.4	0.3
Overstrain in supporting the elderly	26.3	19.2	7.1
Difficulty in controlling and teaching children, mental exhaustion	17.9	20.4	–2.6
Work overload at job	14.7	29.1	–14.4
Difference of opinion between family members, feelings of vexation	11.2	9.1	2.1

Note: Unit: %.

The existence of potential unemployed groups is worth paying attention to. In the survey, there was an urban jobless group and its scale was slightly smaller than the unemployed group. Unlike unemployed people, they expressed that they were not looking for a job and were thus divided into a separate urban jobless group according to the principles for the calculation of unemployment rates and were removed from the economically active population. In the research on unemployment problems, they were often called "potentially unemployed people". This group comprised mainly women (who accounted for 68.1%), with men accounting for 31.9%, and 67.6% had an education level of junior middle school or below, of which 73.3% remained jobless since 2000. In terms of age structure, the urban potentially unemployed group was older, and 58.8% were aged 45 years or older; but the urban unemployed group was mainly 35–49 years old. It can be surmised that after losing their jobs, middle-aged men or young people are inclined to seek a job and become employed; and middle-aged and older women are the main groups that forgo seeking employment and become the potentially unemployed group. The lifestyle of the potential unemployed group is not different from that of the unemployed. Therefore, equal attention must be paid to both groups.

B. *Non-regular employee's social security and employment quality need urgent attention*

In terms of the policy on moderately pushing flexible employment, increasing the flexibility of employment and strengthening the security of employment were the focus points, and the major concerns were the social security and employment quality of the non-regular employed population. According to the survey, the non-regular employed population experiences universally lower social security and wage income and longer working hours.

In terms of the degree of social security, the non-regular employed population had a lower proportion of coverage. In the regular employed group, 62.3% had basic endowment insurance for urban residents, whereas only 19.5% in the non-regular employed group were covered; 67.4% of people had basic medical insurance for urban employees, but only 14.8% in the non-regular employed group were covered; 45.8% of people had unemployment insurance, but only 4.3% in the non-regular employed group were covered; 41.7% of people had workers' compensation insurance, but only 5.2% of the non-regular employed group were covered; 5.4% of people had the urban and rural minimum living security, but 3.4% in the non-regular employed group were covered.

In terms of wages, the regular employed group's average monthly salary was RMB 1,896, while the average monthly salary for the non-regular employed was RMB 1,085; in regular employed people, 17.5% of people's monthly salary was RMB 999 or below, compared to 52.3% in the non-regular employed people.

In terms of weekly working hours, regular employed people's average was 46.25 h, but non-regular employed people averaged 56.91 h. Wu Yaowu and Cai Fang's analysis results also indicated that the average weekly working hours of regular employed people was 42.99 h, whereas that of non-regular employed people was 51.79 h; 89% of regular employed people's working hours were 59 h or lesser, in comparison to only 59.3% for non-regular employed people.

C. Although the employment system of urban and rural isolation has ceased to exist, the employment market of urban and rural division still continues to function

The increase in the universal non-agricultural employment experiences in the rural population have broken the employment system of urban and rural isolation, which has created conditions favorable for rural labor transfer and promoted urbanization construction. However, under the influence of various factors, non-agricultural employment of the rural population has not yet fully realized the transfer of rural labor from rural to urban areas. Through the permeation of rural people working in cities, they finally achieve the transformation from rural population to urban population. Among them, the division of urban and rural employment markets is one of the important reasons.

This employment market of urban and rural division is mainly manifested in two aspects. First, the urban and rural areas are divided into (1) rural employment market, in which the urban population is unwilling to participate in, and (2) the urban employment market, in which the rural population is limited. Urban and rural employment markets are further divided according to regular and non-regular sections, and state-owned (collective) and non-state-owned sections. According to the survey results, urban population held the overwhelming superiority in various domains of urban employment markets, in which the full-time employment proportion

Table 3.5.   Composition of Employment Markets.

		Rural employed people		Urban employed people		Proportion of urban employed people in various employment markets B/(A+B)×100
		Frequency A	Percentage	Frequency B	Percentage	Percentage
Urban employment market	Full-time employment in state-owned sections	23	0.6	548	36.3	96
	Full-time employment in non-state-owned sections	94	2.6	301	19.9	76.2
	Non-regular employment	247	6.7	535	35.5	68.4
Rural employment market	Full-time employment in state-owned sections	44	1.2	21	1.4	32.3
	Full-time employment in non-state-owned sections	248	6.7	25	1.7	9.2
	Non-regular employment	419	11.4	26	1.7	5.8
	Part-time farming	331	9	7	0.5	2.1
	Full-time farming	2,275	61.8	46	3	2
Total		1,659	3,681	100	1,509	100

reached 96% in state-owned (collective) units. Rural population accounted for a large proportion in the rural employment market, but 10% of them participated in urban employment markets, and mainly in non-regular employment domains (see Table 3.5).

The employment market of urban and rural division has restrained the space for the population of rural households to realize employment through non-agriculture jobs. Various factors, including restrictions of the registration system, few employment opportunities in cities, high cost of living, low labor wage, low social position, bad working and living conditions, as well as separation from family, cause workers to return to or remain in their native villages to work in agriculture. In a related survey results, it is estimated by rural family members that 89.7% of migrant laborers who work in a city would go home if they could. About 56.6% of the laborers planned to return to their native villages in the future, and the overwhelming majority of migrant laborers regarded their hometown as their sought-after end result.[4] This has caused the formation of the above-mentioned rural population which mainly comprises middle-aged men who return to their native villages to work in agriculture after leaving their urban jobs.

III. Suggestions on Expanding and Promoting Employment

Since the reforms began 30 years ago, the preliminary establishment of an employment system based on market principles has laid a labor force foundation for China's economic development. With the establishment of this employment system, unceasingly pushing positive employment policy, accelerating the establishment of the social security system on employment, putting forth efforts to improve the employment environment, and further enhancing the quality of labor, China's employment system will one day be fully intact and effective. Owing the influence of the current international financial crisis, China must implement more

---

[4] Li Qiang (李强) (2003). Analyses on driving factors to influence China's urban and rural floating populations. *Chinese Social Science*, Vol. 1, pp. 125.

positive employment policies to overcome the current difficulties in the employment market.

A. *Implementing an economic prosperity plan of employment first*

With the upgrading of industrial structure, the employment elasticity of economic growth continually dropped. In the 1990s, while GDP grew 1%, the total employment increased by about 800,000 people. From 2003, China has entered the "high growth, low employment" phase; the employment elasticity coefficient was 0.1 in 2003, which fell to 0.08 in 2005, and total employment only increased by 630,000 people, while GDP grew 1%. In this case, suitable investment growth plans would be a growth plan of "low employment" or even "without employment". Therefore, the economic prosperity plan of employment should first be implemented to invest in employment; promoting employment should be regarded as the priority target of economic prosperity.

B. *More positive encouragement and normalizing of flexible employment*

Encouraging flexible employment is one measure for various countries to deal with unemployment. In recent years, in some developed countries, the proportion of non-regular employed people in the total population of employed also rose; developing countries regarded promoting flexible employment as the most important means to handle employment. In this survey, at present, non-regular employed workers occupy 49.8% of all non-agricultural employed workers, which indicated that non-regular employment is actually undertaking the heavy responsibility of job enlargement.

For self-employed workers and non-regular employed people, their employment motive is mainly survival needs and is not completely a personal choice; therefore, related policies and measures must be based on low thresholds. Except for the simplification of autonomous management procedures and the deduction and exemption of taxes, the service consciousness of town administration sections should be strengthened to create good conditions for autonomous business operators.

For paid workers in the non-regular employed group, it is important to strengthen the protection of their rights to work. Related research has indicated that since the mid-1990s, labor dispute cases have assumed an upward trend because non-regular employment massively increased and workers' legal rights could not be safeguarded. The worsening working conditions depressed the workers' sense of stable employment, which was also one of primary causes in the rise of short-term unemployment rates.

C. *Taking social significance to transform migrant laborers into new residents seriously*

At present, large or medium-sized cities have become a huge driving force for migrant laborers to settle down and apply in the household registration system and divisional urban and rural employment markets. As a result, the migrant laborers working in cities were unable to settle down and gain employment in large or medium-sized cities, and about one-fourth of migrant laborers ultimately returned to their native villages to work in farms. The changes in the household registration system from the overall reform to the household registration reform of small cities were regarded as the key transfer. The institutional repulsion forces of local cities for migrant laborers working in cities to settle down weakened in the house-hold registration system. This has been helpful for rural residents of non-agricultural employment to leave agricultural jobs and has promoted the synchronized development of rural non-agricultural construction and urbanization.

Other than the first-generation migrant laborers in the early 1990s, who regarded non-agricultural employment as a channel of income increase, farmers working in cities have expected their non-agricultural employment experience to enhance their own lives as well as their children's economic position and social status; movement for employment between the urban and rural areas has started to contain the individual desire to move toward a better standing in society based on the differences between urban and rural areas. In recent years, more children have followed their parents to large or medium-sized cities and enrolled in local compulsory education. This indicated a new generation of migrant laborers hoping to partake in high-quality urban education resources to improve the education conditions for their children. Therefore, realizing settlement in a city through non-agricultural employment has gradually become a component of decision-making for migrant laborers to work in cities.

Under the influence of the global financial crisis, some migrant laborers who originally worked in developed areas started to return to their native homes. Apart from migrant laborers who mainly returned to their native villages to work, some also opted to return to their native provinces, but not their native villages. This raises new questions for rural labors' flow in the future and the pattern of rural labors' unidirectional or multi-stage movement. Settlement in cities promulgated by the traditional theory on urban and rural movement of population may evolve into a pattern of bidirectional ebb and flow. Therefore, on the premise of synchronized improvement of employment policy and employment environment of middle-sized and small towns, this pattern of flowing out and back into settlements will bring new challenges for China's urbanization development.

D. *Taking the development of vocational education, particularly higher vocational education to enhance the quality of labor seriously*

A worker's employment status and quality are closely related to personal education level; simultaneously, the overall quality of labor also decides the quality and scale of social and economic development. Improving the quality of labor is helpful in fundamentally solving the structural problems of the current employment structure. Since the rapid development of general high schools in the 1990s and after general higher education increased recruitment of students, China's vocational education development has faced setbacks: the scale was reduced, the quality of student sources dropped, and teachers left. Although in recent years, vocational education has recovered, as a whole, there has been a certain differential from the requirements of social and economic development. In higher education, while the proportion of elite educational institutions in the form of general colleges and universities is high, the proportion of higher vocational education is conversely small, and while the teaching of subject knowledge was excessively emphasized, the practice was neglected. Therefore, adjusting the higher education structure and speeding up the development

of higher vocational education are the inevitable choices to solve the
employment problems from the angle of sustainable development.

E. *Gradually establishing the monitoring and promulgation system of the investigated unemployment rate*

The unemployment rate is generally regarded as an index that reflects the
overall economic position of a place. In some countries, these social statistics are quite developed; the unemployment rate is often published
every month and is therefore the most sensitive monthly socioeconomic
index in the market. Many countries readjust the interest rate and the wage
prices according to the unemployment rate. The unemployment rate is
also simultaneously a major social indicator and an important basis of
social policy adjustment. Therefore, now most developed countries and
regions announce the unemployment rate every month, and the revised
data every quarter. China should set up a system for monitoring special
urban investigated unemployment rates according to comparable international specifications of unemployment rates to make the unemployment
rate index the main basis of macroscopic policy-making.

Chapter 4

Urban and Rural Residents' Social Security

Zhang Liping

The Chinese economy has experienced high levels of fluctuation as a result of the global financial crisis. It is crucial to accelerate the establishment of a social security system covering urban and rural areas and to perfect various systems for social security in such a way that the social security system can play the role of a "shock absorber" in the economy and act as a "stabilizer" of society by safeguarding basic living standards and consumption of residents and maintaining social harmony and stability.

I. Remarkable Achievements in the Construction of the Social Security System

A. *Frame of social security system covering urban and rural residents has been formed*

In recent years, social security in China has rapidly developed and insisted on the policy of "broad coverage, basic social security, and multi-stratum, sustainable development". A basic framework of social security covering urban and rural residents has been formed. According to the data published by the Ministry of Human Resources and Social Security, by the end of 2008, the population that participated in basic endowment insurance for urban residents, basic medical insurance, and unemployment insurance had reached 219 million, 317 million, and 124 million, respectively.

A social security system that regards systems of endowment insurance, medical service, unemployment, and minimum living security as the core is rapidly developing to become an important guarantee to reach the goal of "universal access to education, reasonable payment for all labors, medical services for all patients, retirement pension provided universally, and affordable housing".

B. *Urban and rural residents' degree of satisfaction with social security has risen*

According to the results of the 2008 national survey, the degree of satisfaction of urban and rural residents with government's work in social security rose obviously, particularly in regard to medical service. The 2008 survey, when compared with similar survey results from 2006, showed that the proportion of urban and rural residents' satisfaction with government's work in social security had risen from 47% in 2006 to 63% in 2008 (see Table 4.1), and the dissatisfaction proportion had dropped from 42% to 31%. Similarly, the proportion of satisfaction with the medical service rose from 58% in 2006 to 72% in 2008 and the proportion of dissatisfaction dropped from 37% to 24%.

Table 4.1. Urban and Rural Residents' Degree of Satisfaction with Government Work in Social Security and Medical Service.

	Providing good medical and health care services		Providing universal social security	
	2006	2008	2006	2008
Very satisfied	6.7	11.9	7.6	11.1
More satisfied	51.1	59.6	39.9	51.4
Less satisfied	28.9	20.4	31.3	24.3
Dissatisfied	8	4	10.4	6.5
Don't know	5.3	3.9	10.8	6.7

Note: Unit: %.

The pressure on residents caused by medical expenditures has been reduced. In the 2006 survey, the cruising data on "pressures of life" showed that 45.5% of residents thought "medical expenditures are too difficult to bear", but in the 2008 survey, this proportion dropped to 37.6%, in which 23.2% of residents thought it was a "huge pressure" and 11.8% thought it provided "some pressure".

C. *Proportion of urban and rural residents who completely pay the medical expenses has dropped largely*

Three safeguard lines, i.e., basic medical insurance for urban employees, medical security for urban residents, and the new rural cooperative medical service, now cover all urban and rural residents in the system. In recent years, the expansion of coverage in the medical security system has progressed with unprecedented speed, which has basically realized the construction of a system of universal coverage.

The rapid advancement of healthcare system construction has made tangible progress. The 2008 survey results showed that the proportion of urban and rural residents who pay for their medical expenses dropped largely. In a similar survey in 2006, for the question, "if you fall sick, who

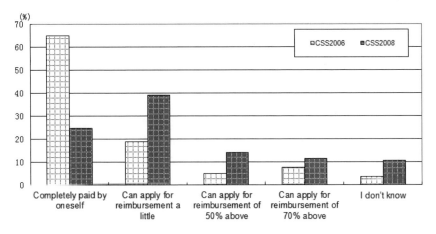

Figure 4.1. Proportion of Urban and Rural Residents' Medical Expenses Paid by Themselves.

pays for the medical expenses"? 65.2% of urban and rural residents answered, "completely pay for medical expenses by oneself"; according to the survey result in 2008, this proportion dropped to 24.7%.

The expansion of coverage of the new rural cooperative medical service has played an obvious role in the higher coverage rates. In the 2006 survey, rural residents' medical expenses "completely paid by themselves" accounted for 72.7%, and urban residents' medical expenses "completely paid by themselves" accounted for 56.6%, in which the proportion that rural residents needed to completely pay medical expenses was largely higher than urban residents. According to the 2008 survey results, the proportion of rural residents fell from 72.7% in 2006 to 17.2% in 2008, and the proportion of urban residents fell from 56.6% in 2006 to 33.1% in 2008.

D. *More migrant laborers now have social security*

Extensive attention has been paid to the social security of migrant laborers. The cruising data showed that the level of participation in the social security system by migrant laborers was varied. In terms of retirement security, they participated in urban and rural endowment insurance and, in the medical service, they participated in not only medical insurance for urban employees and urban residents but also the new rural cooperative medical system. Whether it is the traditional urban or rural security system, all have covered certain proportions of migrant laborers, although, as compared with employed people of non-agricultural household registration, their coverage in the social security system was not yet high but has been distinctly enhanced. This cruising data showed that a high proportion of migrant laborers working in the cities participated in the new rural cooperative medical system, with a coverage rate of 62%. About one-fourth of migrant laborers working in regular sector jobs participated in the medical insurance program for urban employees, about 14% in unemployment insurance, and 36% in workers' compensation insurance. Enabling migrant laborers to be covered by social security is an important act, which may have the same historical significance as cancelling the agricultural tax.

II. Social Security System Needs More Rapid Consummation

China's construction of a social security system is a great achievement, but dealing with economic fluctuation, aging population, population migration, and various employment forms has slowed down the full consummation of the social security system.

A. *Coverage of endowment insurance, particularly of rural endowment insurance, urgently needs to be increased*

Retirement security has been a hotspot of concern, along with the aging population, progressive miniaturization of family structure, and gradual attenuation of family security functions. The traditional family's intergenerational support pattern has been challenged and the urban and rural residents' demands for an urban and rural endowment insurance program have steadily increased. In this survey, retirement security was ranked seventh among the 18 social problems, and 18% of residents thought that retirement security was an important social problem. How to solve problems regarding social security, including retirement security, has immediate influence on the residents' sense of social fairness; in this survey, 50.4% of interviewees thought that social security, including retirement security, were "fair" or "very fair" but almost 40% rated it "very unfair" or "less fair".

From the data of the sampling survey of population changes by the National Bureau of Statistics in 2007, people aged 60 years and older accounted for 13.64% of the total population, and people aged 50 to 59 years also accounted for 13.94%. Solving the problem of retirement security is an important strategy to deal with aging populations. According to the 2008 survey, nearly one-third of families were caring for people aged 60 years and older, in which families caring for one old person accounted for 18% and families caring for two old people surpassed 13%. Overall, 35.2% of old people lived alone, while two-person households accounted for one-third of households surveyed. In terms of income, whether in the

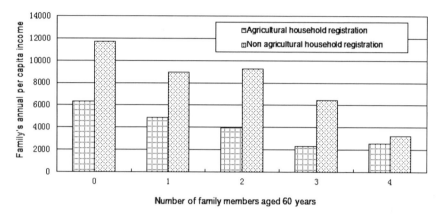

Figure 4.2.   Urban and Rural Household Income and Number of Old Population.

city or countryside, the more seniors in the household, the lower the family's annual per capita income (see Figure 4.2).

According to the 2008 survey, in the 18- to 69-year-old population group of urban household registration, 53% participated in the urban endowment insurance program (including basic endowment insurance for urban residents and the enterprise's supplemental endowment insurance), but in the 18- to 69-year-old population group of rural household registration, only 5.6% participated in the program. China's rural retirement security always gave priority to intrafamilial old age support. After the 1990s, as a result of the practical situation of rural economic development, some areas had established endowment insurance for individual account accumulation according to the principle of "individual payment regarded as the main body and collective subsidies regarded as supplementary while government supports the policy". Afterward, it was compelled to stop because of fund management problems. From 2004, pilot work was carried out in rural one-child families to implement a reward and assistance system: rural one-child or two-girl couples who acted in accordance with the family planning policy were given reward and assistance funds of RMB 600 per annum on average after retirement. Both central and local governments jointly undertook the reward and assistance funds, which elicited a huge response from farmers, but this policy was aimed at the families who carried out family planning policy. By 2006, a total of 1,347,000 people had benefited from this pilot program; however, at present, coverage is still relatively limited. Therefore, after implementing the new rural cooperative medical system and the rural minimum living security system, speeding up the pilot work of the rural endowment insurance and expanding the coverage of rural endowment insurance should be considered.

B. *Solving the problems of medical service is still one of the key points to improve people's livelihood*

The medical services have always been considered, especially by urban residents, to be one of the important issues affecting people's livelihood. In the 2006 survey, "difficulty and expenses to see a doctor" was the social problem that ranked first. Although medical security and medical services has made distinct progress and taken huge strides forward in the recent years, in this 2008 national survey, the problem still ranked second, next to "price rise". In urban and rural areas, 39.6% of urban residents and 44.1% of rural residents believed that "difficulty and expenses to see a doctor" was one of biggest social problems. This problem was manifested in high absolute expenditures for residents to see a doctor. According to a recent related survey, the number of urban and rural low-income families that have fallen into poverty because of medical expenditures have obviously increased. According to the survey results, in terms of the total expenditures of urban and rural household consumption in 2007, medical expenditures accounted for 10.6% of the total expenses, ranking only after food and education expenditures. Among them, urban families' medical expenditures accounted for 9.4% of total expenditures, and absolute medical expenditures were lower for rural families compared to the urban families, but the proportion of total expenditures was higher than that for urban families. Based on different survey specifications, the medical department's data showed that urban residents' healthcare expenditures for the years 1990, 1995, 2000, and 2005 accounted for 2%, 3.1%, 6.4%, and 7.6% of per capita annual consumer expenditures, respectively. In 2006, this proportion started to drop and was 7% in 2007. As compared with other countries and regions, healthcare expenditures in the household consumption were also relatively higher: the healthcare expenditures in the household consumption structure in 2005 for Britain, France, Germany, and Italy were 1.6%, 3.4%, 4.6%, and 3.2%, respectively.

C. *Coverage of unemployment insurance should be further expanded*

From the mid-1990s until now, the total laid-off and unemployed populations have increased, and there was a sudden spurt in urban registered unemployed population, numbering 8 million people every year in the last five years.

The coverage of current unemployment insurance is still small, and some unemployed people could not be rescued by unemployment insurance. For the registered unemployed people, whether in re-employment, self-employment, or in retirement, preferential policy related to medical insurance has been implemented. For unemployed people without registration, for example, the staffs of some restructured state-owned enterprises lost their jobs not because the enterprises halted production but because the enterprise did not yet go bankrupt, and though they were not laid-off, they were still not able to work. Therefore, their wages have been stopped and they are unable to enjoy the minimum living security. Some off-production enterprises did not pay for unemployment insurance and, therefore, their labor force is unable to have coverage of unemployment insurance. In brief, at present, quite a substantial part of the actual unemployed population is not covered by unemployment insurance compensation and is also not counted in the unemployment statistics.

According to the cruising data in 2008, for 18- to 60-year-old urban unemployed population, the proportion of participation in endowment insurance was 31.3% and the proportion covered by medical insurance was 37.4%; however, the proportion covered by unemployment insurance was only 6.1%, and a mere 5% were covered by the urban minimum living security program. According to the survey, for unemployment insurance, different types of enterprises had different proportions of participation. The highest proportion to participate in the unemployment insurance was in the state-owned enterprises, at 58.1%; next was in the cooperative ventures and solely foreign-funded enterprises, at 36%; and 28.4% in collective enterprises; but the coverage of unemployment insurance in mass-run non-enterprise organizations and private enterprises was only slightly higher than 12%. The surveyed coverage rate of unemployment insurance was lower than the data published by the national statistics department mainly because of different statistical specifications and because different types of enterprises and migrant laborers were included in the cruising data.

D. Consummating the social insurance system of non-public enterprises and of non-regular employed people

According to the survey, the participation rate in social security was still related to the nature of employment units, and public enterprises had higher participation degree in the social security than non-public enterprises. The cruising data showed that, in the current employed population aged 18 to 60 years old, there was more endowment insurance coverage in the public enterprises, cooperative ventures, and solely foreign-funded enterprises. For instance, in state-owned and collective enterprises, the coverage of urban endowment insurance was 60–80%, and nearly 60% in cooperative ventures and solely foreign-funded enterprises; in private enterprises, only 33% of employed people participated had endowment insurance coverage, and only about 17% were in individual enterprises and without stable working units. For workers such as freelance and casual laborers, who were not part of traditional working units, the endowment insurance coverage was basically the same as that of small businessmen, at about 17%.

In different types of enterprises, the coverage of medical security was 65% to 90%, but in state-owned and state-owned holding enterprises, collective enterprises and cooperative ventures, and solely foreign-funded enterprises, staffs mainly participated in the medical insurance for urban employees; the insured rate was 69%, 47.8%, and 43%, respectively. Staffs in private enterprises and in the mass-run non-enterprise organizations, as well as small businessmen, mainly participated in the new rural cooperative medical service. There was a low proportion of medical insurance coverage for urban employees; particularly, more than 50% of small businessmen participated in the new rural cooperative medical service, but only 5.4% of urban employees were covered. In addition, 12.5% participated in medical insurance for urban residents (see Figure 4.3).

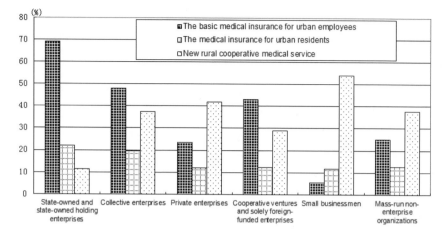

Figure 4.3. Medical Insurance of Staffs in Different Types of Enterprises.

E. *Attention should be paid to the age of the insured people*

Along with economic and social development, the improvement of living standards, and the enhancement of medical technology and resident's per capita life expectancy also increased; the age structure has shifted to an older majority, the absolute population of old people is rapidly increasing, the family's elder dependency coefficient is enhancing, and the social burden of retirement security, medical security, as well as corresponding social utilities used by old population is also increasing. The insured people's age structure is gradually becoming older, the payment pressure of social security funds is increasing, and the problem of structural aging has become a crucial point of research. Taking the data of participation in the basic endowment insurance as the example, in the early 1990s, the ratio between the insured active staffs and the retired staffs was 5.4:1; by the mid-1990s, it rose to 4:1, while in 2007, the rate fell to 3.06:1.

This cruising data also showed that in terms of basic medical insurance for urban employees and basic endowment insurance for urban residents, the prevailing trend was that social security coverage is increasing with age. The insured rate of social security decreased successively along with the reduction of age, particularly, in the age group of 50 years and above. This means that the endowment insurance fund dependency coefficient gradually increases once income from endowment insurance funds fall below expenditures, an immediate influence brought to the service and function of endowment insurance system (see Table 4.2).

III. Suggestions on Consummating the Social Security System

Under the current background of the global economic crisis, promoting consumption, expanding domestic demand, and driving economic growth have become universal goals in China. The uncertainty of future retirement

Table 4.2.   Insured Proportion of Urban Residents in Different Age Groups in the Urban Social Security.

Age group	Basic endowment insurance for urban residents	Enterprise's supplement endowment insurance (including enterprise annuity)	Basic medical insurance for urban employees (including socialized medicine)	Medical insurance for urban residents	Sample size
18–19 years old	11.2	1.1	6.7	26.7	89
20–24 years old	19.9	4.3	16.8	18.3	186
25–29 years old	36.7	14	30.2	18.7	215
30–34 years old	42.9	9.7	38.2	19.7	259
35–39 years old	43.5	13.8	37.1	25.2	333
40–44 years old	42.3	14.7	37.2	23.7	333
45–49 years old	50.7	17.2	46.5	26.4	274
50–54 years old	53.4	18	51.3	20.6	268
55–59 years old	55.8	15.8	57.2	23.7	215
60–64 years old	59.3	10.7	55.1	23.8	167
65–69 years old	55.4	24.8	55.5	22.5	139

Note: Unit: %, person.

and medical and education costs are affecting family savings and has suppressed normal consumer expenditures. Therefore, only after eliminating this uncertainty can personal consumption be promoted. In recent years, coverage of social security has expanded rapidly and the pressures of medical service and retirement security on resident's life have dropped; more families have the ability to avoid the risks of life through the establishment of a social security system. Through further consummation of the social security system, families' woes about normal expenses should be eliminated gradually, allowing anticipated consumption to be stabilized and consumer confidence to be strengthened, thus increasing the domestic demand.

A. *Further consolidating urban and rural development achievements of social security and earnestly improving the capacity of social security*

Through great efforts over several years, the coverage of social security has been expanded rapidly, but further efforts are needed to consolidate this achievement. The social security level should be enhanced so that the insured people can really profit from it, and an incentive mechanism of continuous payment and participation should be established. Resident's expenditure ability from social security funds should be increased through the expansion of coverage to reach the requirements for the "law of large number" of insurance so that the social security system can develop healthily. Simultaneously, publicity on the various policies on social security should be strengthened to enhance the awareness rate; through the survey, we discovered that over 15% of people participating in medical insurance programs did not know the proportion of reimbursement they received. This scenario indicated that, while expanding the coverage of social security, more careful work should be done so that residents can understand what benefits they can obtain by participating in insurance programs. Moreover, with the unceasing consummation of the social security system and the unceasing expansion of coverage, the group being served is increasing, and the mission of undertaking and management services for the social security is likewise increasing. To meet the requirements of the new situation and mission, the supervisor level should be improved, and service should be promoted to adapt to the transforming group that is insured.

B. *Speeding up the implementation of rural endowment insurance and reducing older resident's dependency*

The current social security system is mainly designed, managed, and operated according to two kinds of urban and rural socioeconomic formations; the urban and rural dualistic structure is obvious. After the basic framework of urban social security system is established, the construction of the rural social security system should be put on the main agenda of policymakers. A new rural social endowment insurance system urgently needs to be established to solve problems regarding retirement security and medical services for farmers in the new rural cooperative medical system; the pilot work of rural endowment insurance voluntarily organized in various areas also needs instruction and support from solid national policy. At present, in some developed rural areas, the opportunity for the construction of a basic retirement security system has matured, and solving the problems of rural retirement security should be regarded as an important step for eradicating the urban/rural dualistic structure and for realizing urban and rural integration.

C. *Paying attention to the social security of migrant laborers and non-regular employed people*

Migrant laborers have low coverage rates in programs, including social security; their awareness of programs is low and they lack initiative to seek them. Employers are often not willing to insure employees against the social security system, and the present system is not suitable for migrant laborers' actual employment status. Transfer and connection between employers are not smooth, and enforcement is also weak. Based on the current stage of economic development and the next goal, the construction of an urban and rural social security system should be considered as a whole. A social security system that may link urban and rural areas and that conforms to migrant laborers' characteristics of movement should be designed to establish a nationwide unified social security system for migrant laborers.

D. *Expanding insured coverage rates and improving the insured crowd's age structure*

The growth of the aging insured population requires a new optimization in structure to establish a multi-level social security system to expand the insured crowd from the original urban staffs to universal coverage. Policy-makers should aim to design different levels of medical insurance projects to adapt different levels of crowds and to expand the insured proportion of in-service staffs, and young people to further optimize the insured people's age structure and to delay the process of the insured pool's aging structure.

The 17th National Congress of the Communist Party of China had explicitly put forward the goal to basically establish a social security system covering urban and rural residents up to 2020. The year 2008 was an extraordinary year for the construction of the social security system. At the beginning of the year, the release of the insurance law draft, new medical reform program, the institution retirement security reform, and the pilot work of new rural endowment insurance all indicated that the construction of the social security system entered a new and crucial phase. It is definite that along with the increase of the strength of social security system reform and the unceasing expansion of coverage, more and more people will profit from it, which would play an irreplaceable role for the improvement of the people's livelihood and the expansion of domestic demand. At present, in the situation where the economy faces huge difficulties, financial revenue growth is blocked and various aspects need huge investment. The normal development of social security needs to be maintained because the consummation of a social security system can stabilize domestic consumption and can help China reach the goal of expanding domestic demand and promoting economic growth.

Chapter 5

Urban and Rural Residents' Social Support

Diao Pengfei

Along with the advancement of globalization, industrialization, and marketing, various social risks are also substantially increasing; these risks include not only traditional social risks, such as aging, disease, disability, death, as well as various natural disasters, but also unemployment, poverty, injury on the job, and safety violations in industry. New social risks, such as financial crises, stock market crashes, environmental pollution, food safety, and extreme urbanization, have also become a problem (Li Peilin, 2006). These risks have gone beyond individual and family resistance in many situations and, therefore, exterior support and policy assistance are required. This exterior support and assistance comes in three forms: system security provided by the government; diverse paid services provided by the market; and "social support" other than the national safeguards and market services. This generalized "social support" may include family support, support from relatives and friends, social cooperation, community support, and support from social organizations, all of which are important to construct an effective social support network and to help individuals and families avoid the aforementioned social risks.

Social support is prominent in periods of social transition. During market reforms, system safeguards and the organized support formed under the original planned economy become less effective and new institutional and other support systems need time to grow and mature. In the transformation process from work unit security to social security, from work units "undertaking social responsibility" to the community's autonomous organizations, and from a social life depending on employers to depending on community (Li Peilin, 2001), the social security system and community organizations should continue the former functions of work units. These services not only need massive investment of material and human resources as well as organizational framework construction but also need relevant individual study to effectively adapt new institutional arrangements. This process of modernization reforms actually places less importance on familial ties and more on community presence. The growth of social and regional movements has changed a relatively steady environment of interpersonal interaction in urban and rural dwelling units. A number of questions arise with regard to the process of marketization and modernization, such as the changes that may ensue due to shift in social support and the pressures and challenges that may be brought about by transition between new and old systems?

Under the current background of natural disasters and the international financial crisis, the construction of a social support network becomes even more important. Therefore, understanding the present situation of various support sources obtained by urban and rural residents during social reforms, analyzing its development trend, and exploring ways to build a new social support net become important realistic topics.

Research on social support has become a subject of interdisciplinary study across community psychology, epidemiology, and mental health, from the 1970s until now. Early studies focused on the role of "reducing valves" and "buffer" through social support to alleviate individual pressure and to maintain individual health (Cassel, 1976; Cobb, 1976). At that time, researchers mainly defined the social support from the standpoint of psychology and thought that social support included being loved, being respected, and the sense of group belonging, and individual feelings outweighed the influence reality had on the individual (Cobb, 1976). From the 1980s, researchers introduced analysis concepts and methods of social networking into the social support domain (Wellman, 1981); studies on social support networks redefined social support from the angle of social networks and gradually established its dominant position in the studies on social support. At that time, studies on social support often exchanged concepts of social relations, social networks, and social support and mainly focused on the existence, quantity, and contact frequency of social relations (House *et al.*, 1988). This generation of studies on social support showed that the social support network was a network of interpersonal relationships that displayed positive functions and further showed that social support was embodied in interpersonal interaction, the source of aid and assistance (Antonucci and Knipscheer, 1990).

To survey social support networks, different researchers use different tools and points of measurement. One general measuring method is, in view of several kinds of supports (such as emotion, borrowing money, and family affairs), to ask for a list of people who provide support (Fischer, 1982); another method is to ask for a list of people who may provide support (Burt, 1984; Marsden, 1987). At present, studies on social support have developed items, compared to many countries, and the international comparative studies have propelled studies on standardization and acculturation of support based on the network survey (see international social survey project, ISSP).

In studies on the Chinese society, scholars have paid typical attention to the support of "relations" in practice or emotion as one kind of non-regular support resource. Existing empirical studies on specific areas or specific crowds have indicated that the network of social relations may become an important way to obtain the scarce resources (Xiong Ruimei (熊瑞梅) and Huang Yizhi (黄毅志) 1992; Li Peilin (李培林) 1996; Bian Yanjie (边燕杰) 1997; Bian Yanjie and Zhang Wenhong (张文宏) 2001) and beneficial safeguard to maintain physical and intellectual integrity [He Zhaiping (贺寨平) 2004; Lee *et al.*, 2005; Zhao Yandong (赵延东) 2007]. Increasing number of studies have shown that the network of social relations has explanatory abilities in many domains. However, at present, nationwide sampling surveys of social support networks are lacking. The representative samples obtained through sampling surveys of specific cities and specific areas describe the structure and composition characteristics of Chinese people's typical discussion networks and have analyzed the social macrostructure factors that affect an individual's personal networks (Ruan Danqing *et al.*, 1990; Ruan *et al.*, 1997; Zhang Wenhong (张文宏) and Ruan Danqing, 1999).

This study profited from former research findings of sampling surveys of personal networks and described the basic status of Chinese urban and rural residents' individual support networks using the data information of "The CSS" (2008). This survey measured the social support obtained by individuals using name-generator methods. In terms of practical measurements, interviewers recorded the number of people and organizational frameworks that provided assistance for the interviewees for the past one year and then asked for detailed personal information of the first five supporters as well as the information of the first three organizational frameworks.[1]

I. Status and Characteristics of Social Support

A. *Organized support changes from "work unit" to "community"*

In a planned economy, some "unit organizations" such as government-sponsored institutions, state-owned enterprises, and institutionalized people's communes are the main sources of organized support. These are also the foundation of the government's social management, and support for housing, welfare, mutual aid, poverty alleviation, and conflict settlement are all carried out through "unit organizations" (Lu Feng (路风), 1989; Li Peilin and Zhang Yi (张翼), 2000). In the urban planned economy system prior to the reforms, work units were the providers of institutional and organizational safeguards. Living resources of urban employees and their family were mainly provided by their work unit; employees' healthcare, financial difficulties, domestic disputes, and personal psychological issues were solved through the work unit and the work unit's party organization.

---

[1] Interviewees' nomination to organizational support in survey includes government agencies and for-profit agencies; strictly speaking, the assistance provided by these two types of organizations cannot fall under social support. However, comparing the difference between the assistance of these two types of organizations and social organizations is one of the important subjects in the studies; therefore, we contain the support of all types of organizational frameworks for the individual into the concept of organizational support in the analyses in this chapter.

Simultaneously, the work unit also provided education and medical services for employees' children. Therefore, having a good work unit (institution or collective enterprise) or a spouse working in a good work unit was the key to secure good fortune. After the reform and opening up, an important change in the social domain has been the status change of members of different social classes from "work unit staff" to "social beings", along with a massive increase of social movement (Li Peilin, 2001). The coverage of the system of units has been reduced, the number of employed people outside "work units" has largely increased, and the reforms in the systems of employment, medical services, and retirement pensions have gradually changed the face of social services and welfare provided mainly by the work unit to the society as a whole.

According to the findings, support provided by the work unit (the organizations and agencies from which interviewees had accepted assistance in the past one year, including the work unit of interviewees and their relatives), only accounted for 6.3%, whereas the support provided by the community (village committee, residents' committee) occupied over two-fifths of all organized supports (Figure 5.1). The practice of people seeking

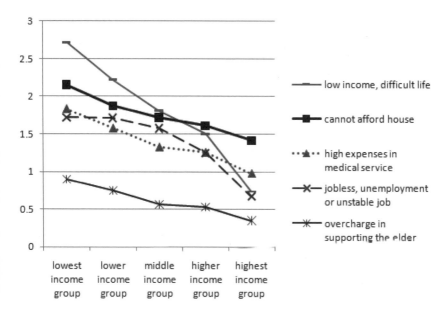

Figure 5.1. Proportion of Support Provided by Different Organizations.

solutions from the work unit for a problem under the planned economy has transformed into one of asking for solutions from the community, under the market economy. The work unit has ceased to be the main factor in people's life and support; employee benefits originally provided by the work unit have become provisions of social organization and systems. The transformation from "the work unit undertaking social responsibility" to "the community serving the society" has made the community the supplier of most support in the social lives of those in the community.

Certainly, working personnel in different units obtain different sources of organized support (see Figure 5.2). According to the analysis of findings, after the reform and opening up, in the category of newly created employment, such as the rural household operations, small businesses, private enterprises, cooperative ventures, and solely foreign-funded enterprises, the employed group obtain more support from the community (community support accounts for more than 40%). On the contrary, in official work "units", such as state-owned and collective enterprises, and state-owned and public institutions, the support obtained by the staff of "work units" was more than from the "community". Party and government organizations are exceptions: the proportion of their employees depending on community support was lowest in work sectors and, simultaneously, did not depend on work units. This may be because of the implementation of the system of public service, and more perfect institutional safeguard have been established to form the current support of a national safeguard system of "community support".

As a whole, "work units" no longer act as the leader in the organized support of the entire society, and diverse and social supports based on the community play leading roles. For the interviewees working in non–state-owned units, their organized support mainly comes from the community, and the support from the work unit has significantly diminished. In the traditional work unit under the "system of units" — the state organs, the state-owned enterprises, and government institutions — the work unit's organized support for employees on an average accounted for about 22% of services. As for the employed people in these organizations, a part of support that "system of units" attenuates is shared by the community, the local government, the party, mass organizations, the social group, and the marketability organization. However, the community support occupied less than 20% in these

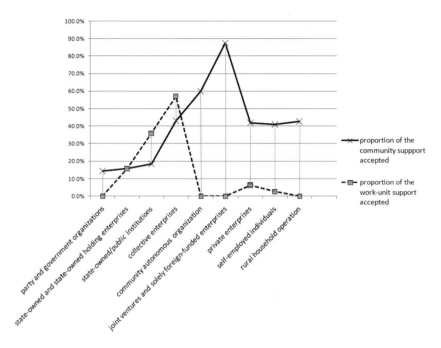

Figure 5.2.   Proportion of the Community Support and the Unit Support Accepted by the People Employed in Different Work Units.

organized supports of employees under the original "system of units", which were lower than the support functions of work units. It can be said that, although the system of units gradually weakened as a whole, employees in the unit still maintained their dependence on the unit.

B. *Low-income groups obtain the most individual and organized supports*

According to the analysis of the findings, a family's per capita income assumes an inverse correlation with the quantity of organized support. The lower the household income, the more is the quantity of organized support obtained (Pearson product-moment correlation coefficient $r = -0.057$, $p < 0.01$). Through five equal groups of per capita income of a family, as compared with the quantity of organized support among groups, the result of one-factor analysis of variance showed that income assumed an inverse correlation with the organized support mainly because the quantity of organized support obtained by 20% of the group with lowest per capita income was obviously more than the other income groups. Except the lowest per capita income group, other four income groups did not have a big difference in the quantity of organized support. The income grouping material showed that the object of organized support increased in low-income groups.

Moreover, the family's per capita income grouping also assumed an inverse correlation with the quantity of individual support. The quantity of individual support obtained by the 20% of lowest-income group was obviously more than other four income groups. Besides the lowest-income group, the other four income groups did not have a distinct difference in the quantity of individual support. This finding shows that the resources of individuals and organized supports lay particularly in the 20% with the lowest income (see Figure 5.3).

C. *Economic support is still the most main type of support*

Besides comparing the quantity of support, we also compared the type of support accepted by the respondents. The support obtained by individuals varied; it included lending money or goods, emotional assistance, and

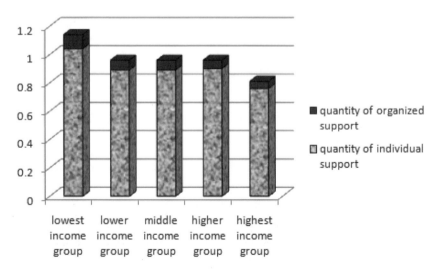

Figure 5.3.   Supports Obtained by Different Per Capita Income Groups of Family.

help for important matters. In our analysis, the supports were divided into four types: the economic support, the expressive support, and support for important matters. The analysis results showed that the economic support was still the most important type of support. According to the five income groups, other than the highest-income group, the three main types of support were financial, psychological, and important affairs; the financial class was the main support, but financial supports obtained by various income groups decreased successively in turn from the lowest income group to the highest income group (see Figure 5.4). In contrast, psychological support decreased successively in turn from the highest income group to the lowest income group as a whole. This reflected how social supports meet different demands of different income groups.

D. *Urban and rural residents' support networks have obvious differences*

The survey results showed that, whether in terms of individual support or organized support, there were obvious differences between urban and rural residents' support networks. In the difference, we saw some groups maintaining tradition structures of support, namely the close contact

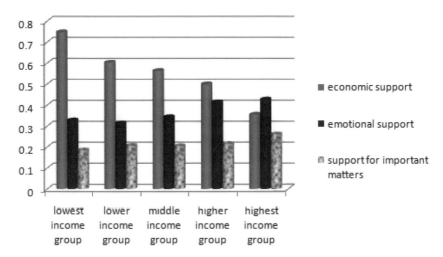

Figure 5.4. Three Types of Supports Obtained by Different Per Capita Income Groups of Family

of family relationships and mutual supports. We also saw the tendency of the scale of individual support networks reducing in the process of modernization and urbanization, the scope of relatives who could provide the support was also reducing; however, the proportion of non-relative support was increasing.

In the individual support network, rural residents have bigger individual support networks than urban residents and rely more on familial support structures. However, both rural and urban residents' individual support networks were mainly composed of kinship support and the proportion of kinship relations was 77.8% and 72.6%, respectively. Moreover, the kinship support in rural individual support networks was the means of expansion to support kinship relations, from spouses, children, and parents, to spouse's parents, daughters-in-law, and sons-in-law, etc. Because rural blood relationships, marital relationships, and geographical relationships are often fixed in a limited spatial scale, the kinship that villagers may maintain is more widespread. The kinship relations in urban individual support networks concentrate on the interior nuclear family (such as the conjugal relation and the parent-child relationship). Moreover, in China's eastern, central, and western regions, the higher the level of urbanization, the greater is the resident's individual support network concentrated on the interior nuclear family. The process of industrialization and urbanization is often followed by the miniaturization and nuclearization of the family; the nuclear family gradually becomes independent of expanded kinship relations in the urbanization process and relatives' support also slowly draws back into the small family, which will become the future trend of development. On the contrary, the proportion of non-kinship relations in urban residents' individual support networks was obviously higher than that in rural residents. In rural areas, the clustering of blood relationships, marital relationships, and common occupations among relatives has made it easy for the rural residents to conveniently seek the support of kinship relations when facing difficulties. In cities, the clustering degree of kinship relations is lower than rural areas; urban residents' occupations are diverse, and the opportunity for relatives to be engaged in the same occupation is lesser than in rural areas. Therefore, as compared with rural residents, urban residents possibly obtain support from non-kinship relations when facing difficulties.

In terms of organized support, urban residents under the original planned economy depended on the work unit, the party, and mass organizations, as the socialization and marketization level of the organized supports was not high (see Figure 5.5). First, we observe the similarity of urban and rural organized support networks: support quantity does not have a distinct difference. Whether in the city or in the countryside, the most important organized support comes from the community (residents' committee/villagers' committee), which occupies 41.7% and 43.3% of urban and rural organized support resources, respectively. Another significant source of assistance is the local government sector, which occupies, respectively, 22.4% and 30.4% of social security assistance. Other than these common grounds, the difference between urban and rural organized support was characterized by urban residents relying more on the party, mass organizations, and the work unit. As compared with the city, the countryside lacked the work unit channel of organized support, and the party and mass organizations were less developed than the city. The data showed that the work unit, the party, and mass organizations only accounted for 1.8% and 6.7% of rural organized support, but the function of the work unit and the party and mass organizations in the city was largely higher than the village, and provided 10.2% and 15.0% of organized supports, respectively. In terms of market support sources, villages

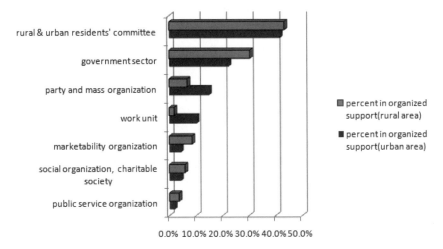

Figure 5.5.   Urban and Rural Organized Supports.

provided 8.5% of organized supports through market organizations based on banks (credit cooperatives), which were higher than the city. Villages provided social support slightly more than the city by the mass organization based on professional associations and guilds. It is observed that, in the market reforms, the villages with weak original planned economies went ahead of the rest, and their level of organized support sources are the highest; in some areas, urban residents still seek the support of their original work units and of the party and mass organizations.

The comparative results of urban and rural support networks showed that, from the tradition to the modern, from the planned economy to the market economy, two kinds of social change processes act on people's livelihoods in reforms. In the transformation from a traditional acquaintance society to a modern society, the kinship relation is not discarded, although contact among relatives has inevitably been reduced, the support and mutual aid among close relatives is still maintained; although modern city life lets people have more contact opportunities outside relatives, people who can provide support are still concentrated in familial relationships. In the process of market reforms, the new support forms cannot mature overnight; for common residents, they need to study and adapt to build a support network and to avoid the risks of transfer between modern and traditional systems.

II. Issues in the Social Support System

Through analysis, we saw that, during these huge social changes, new support systems are growing and replacing the original support system, but still there are problems.

A. *Coverage of social support needs to be increased*

According to the findings, residents who received organized support in the prior year comprised only 6.2% of the interviewees, in which the overwhelming majority (92.5%) obtained the help of one organization. The function of "work unit" safeguards has gradually weakened and it accounted less than 7% of all organized supports, and quite a large number of people cannot join these official safeguards. Moreover, organized support is mostly concentrated in financial support, including direct grants on grain, subsidies for families, minimum living security, and financial disaster relief. In this survey, people who were 70 years or older were excluded; if considering this group's demand for life care, the gap of support including life-support services was more distinct.

B. *Organized support still mainly depends on local government*

Residents who have formerly obtained support from the work unit have now transferred the responsibility to social and marketability organizations. At present, these organizations should also be cultivated, and the cruising data showed that social and charitable organizations occupied only 5% of all organized support, and market-based organizations accounted for only 6.3%. Data from the *China Social Statistical Yearbook* in 2008 showed that, since entering the new century, social organizations have had considerable development, in which the quantity of non-enterprises and foundations grew quickly. However, the function in social services was also extremely limited. The resources required for the organized support still mainly depended on local government allocation.

C. *Social support network excessively relies on personal relations*

According to the findings, interviewees who accepted other extensive individual support in the past one year accounted for 38.5% of total subjects, which largely surpassed the coverage of organized supports; people in the transition period depended more on the personal relations to obtain support. Of the interviewees who obtained individual support, nearly 60% obtained the support of two or more people. The analysis of the characteristics of support providers in the individual support network showed that the individual support network was a small-scale network in which relatives are dominant and which was composed of people with frequent contact; the overwhelming majority (93% of supporters) was closely acquainted with the interviewees.

There are also increasing costs in terms of maintaining an acquaintance relation network. The survey showed that household expenditures toward human relationships are positively correlated with the quantity of individual support. The more the support obtained by an interviewee, the higher were the family expenses used in the human relationship (Pearson product-moment correlation coefficient $r = 0.038$, $p < 0.01$). The expenditure for human relationships accounts for a high proportion of family expenditures, particularly in the rural areas. We further analyze the relation between expenditures for human relationships and the pressure caused by "greater expenditures for human relationships". The results showed that the higher the proportion of the expenditures for human relationship in total family expenditures, the bigger was the pressure on expenditures for human relationship (Pearson product-moment correlation coefficient $r = 0.265$, $p < 0.01$). Rural residents maintained bigger individual support networks than urban residents, and the corresponding expenditures for human relationship accounted for high proportions in total family expenditures. Originally, the individual support network featured high flexibility and low costs, which can play a positive role in meeting demands and prompt support;

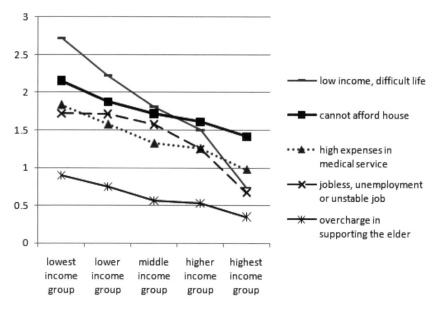

Figure 5.6.   Residents' Pressure on Life by Five Income Groups.

however, excessive dependence on the individual support network caused excessive high costs of social support to reduce pressure and burden on the people who require support.

D. *Low-income families still faces bigger pressures on life*

Although the quantity of individual support and organized support obtained by the lowest income group was higher than other income groups, we must see that the social support obtained by the low-income families was still insufficient. The financial pressure felt by the lowest income group was largely higher than other four groups. These pressures included "bad housing conditions, cannot afford house", "high expenses in medical services", "joblessness, unemployment, or unstable jobs", "overcharging in supporting elders", and "contradiction between family members, be vexed" (see Figure 5.6). More than that, the lowest income groups also felt more pressure in "overcharges in expenditures for human relationships" than the other income groups. The existing personal individual support cannot effectively alleviate the pressures of low-income families.

As compared with the other four income groups, the lowest income families not only had big pressures in life but also had low institutional safeguard levels. This group of interviewees had the following character- istics: the average age was the highest of five income groups, most were married to in-service staff, the average education level was the lowest of the five groups (90% at junior middle school below, 60% at elementary school below), most were agricultural workers (81%) and industrial workers (6.6%), the work unit was mainly the non-regular employment sector (85% in rural household operation and 12% in private enterprises, self-employed businesses, cooperative ventures, and solely foreign-funded enterprises); and most received subsidies (65%) and came from high-debt families (57%). In this income group, the "new rural cooperative medical system" was the most accepted form of social security, and other social security coverage levels were less than 5%. Low-income families have high financial pressure in life and low social security coverage levels; the available resources are not enough when they encounter diseases and unemployment. Even with the individual support provided by the family, they often still cannot effectively solve their problems.

III. Suggestions on Constructing the Social Support Network

A. *Strengthening community construction*

Basic community organization occupies an important position in the official support resource disposition. However, at present, autonomous community organizations are in a passive operating state characterized by "various higher systems and various higher departments which have their own standards and specific job requirements, basic-unit organization must be implemented well" and does not form "specialized" organization troops that community work depends on. Moreover, in recent years, the statistical data showed that the quantity of villagers' (urban residents') committees and their memberships have largely declined. If new programs purely depend on existing community resources to undertake social service functions transferred from the government, the tightness of money and the shortage of professional staff are endemic. Therefore, community construction should regard socialized service network centers as the carriers, depending on the community to raise the public service level and providing rescue to integrate the support resources and to help residents build a system of "helping people to help themselves" for a social support network. According to the actual conditions of various areas, this requires government investment to mobilize the units inside and outside the community, the social organizations, and volunteers and to develop a community service network so that the community can become a "transfer station" of welfare resources which integrates resources and serves residents.

B. *Positively pushing social work and cultivating the specialized organization of social services*

Social work is a kind of important carrier and implementation means to innovate within China's social management system since it vigorously pushes the idea and method of social work in the social management domain. This is an inevitable choice to adapt China's social development changes and is also a symbol for modern social management to gradually mature. Social work plays a vital role in helping the poor and disenfranchised by providing all kinds of personalized social supports. We must cultivate a huge specialized group of social workers and specialized organizations of social work, develop specialized organization of social work and many channels of cooperation in training organization, and fully optimize existing community service facilities and resources to construct a social support network that meets the demands of social development. The development of social work should be vigorously supported with tax revenue, specialized technical qualifications, and education training and employment.

C. *Continuing to play support role of work unit*

In the process of marketization, the role of the work unit has had a big transformation in terms of organized support, but we could see that unit support is still playing a positive role in the current reforming transition period. As compared with the support provided by local governments and other organizations, in the support provided by the work unit, the highest proportion of support simultaneously covers the financial, psychological, and other supports needed. The work unit can comprehensively and promptly understand the difficulties of individuals and provide help when needed. It is, however, difficult for social groups and government departments to understand individuals in detail, and they often provide singular support. At present, the institutional and organization security systems are also immature, and the community service network which meets residents' demands needs to be further constructed. In the social reforming period, the role of social support provided by work units is still important.

D. *Constructing widespread coverage of social security and public service systems*

Although for individuals, in essence, the social support network is indispensable, existing social support relies excessively on the individual support provided by personal relationships, which cannot effectively alleviate the pressures of low-income families and people. As for the entire social stratification, it is more important to avoid the risks of life by relying on the institutional safeguards and the service system. China must aim to establish perfect widespread coverage of social security systems and strengthen public service systems, including healthcare, employment, and retirement support. Social security, public service system, and social support system are the three major pillars of the social safety net. Formerly, the organized support that depended on work units or the individual support that depended upon kinship relations brought about excessive dependence, shortages of resources, and the insufficient support. We suggest great attention be paid to mutual cooperation among institutional safeguards, the public service system, and the social support system, thereby enhancing the ability of the entire society to deal with risks and safeguard China as a prosperous harmonious society of solidarity, mutual aid, and mutual confidence.

Chapter 6

Evolution Process and the Trend of Income Differential

Chen Guangjin

Domestic and foreign academic circles have heavily researched China's income disparity; generally, all research conclusions show that since the reform and opening up, the income differentials have presented a tendency of unceasing expansion. The difference has been mainly concentrated on the method to judge the social and economic significance of this differential; for example, whether the existing differential has been overstated, whether to present the polarization, whether China displays a Kuznets' inverted U curve, how will the income differentials evolve in the future, and other questions of this nature.

I. Questions Researched and Proposed Hypotheses

China's income differential has become staggering; irrespective of how we understand the causality, this is an undeniable fact. The questions at hand are: How did this huge differential evolve? What characteristic and nature does its evolutionary process have? How will the differential evolve in the future? These questions are not only the focus of academic research but also major issues concerning the whole of Chinese society. Academic circles have carried out a great deal of research on this topic and have raised many competitive theories and viewpoints.

Different countries' income differentials have experienced their own evolution patterns during different periods. With these income differential patterns, what is more important is the popularization between the rich and poor contained in this situation. For example, Kuznets discovered that, in the 50 years before the Second World War, the developed countries' income differential had experienced a process of an inverted U curve (Kuznets, 1955); other scholars' research discovered that, from the late-1960s, the income differentials of major Western countries presented inverted U curve-shaped changes (Alderson *et al.*, 2005). Speaking of China, under the situation of increasing income differentials, the question is whether this trend will be followed or whether further polarization might occur. Due to China's circumstances, this question is worth studying. The related research of domestic academic circles has raised all sorts of views, and they may be roughly divided into three kinds of major viewpoints.

According to the first viewpoint, China does not truly have income polarization. This viewpoint is mainly based on two postulates. The first is that present-day China's income differential appears based on the overall income level and not on the basis that the rich is richer, and the poor is poorer, therefore, we cannot think that China's income differential has presented polarization. Even with a high degree of income differential, there is no indication that the polarization has truly occurred (Chen Zongsheng (陈宗胜), 1997; Wang Minghua (王明华), 2003. The second kind of basis lies in logic theory. Some scholars cited the Kuznets hypothesis and believed that China's expansion of income differential is a normal phenomenon in the process of market economic development; therefore, it is unnecessary to become alarmed. Some scholars cited related discussions of Marx and Deng Xiaoping (邓小平) and thought that the polarization was defined demonstrably by Marx and Deng Xiaoping; they theorized that this occurrence is in association with the private ownership of the means of production, a commodity economy, and the exploitation of working classes. Therefore, the polarization is a concept of social class and at present China does not have polarization at quite this scale of significance (Su Xiaoli (苏晓离), 1996; Jin Xizai (金喜在), 1996; Wang Minghua (王明华), 2003; Zhu Hongjun (朱红军), 2007; Ning Deye (宁德业) and Pang Yejun (庞业君), 2007).

The second viewpoint believes that, at present, China has serious polarization of income distribution. These researchers put aside class differentiation, and the analysis focused on the income distribution patterns and its changing processes. Certainly, among them were also specific theories and values. Some scholars believe that, in the situation where related national policy has been insufficiently reasonable, the development of a market economy will continuously and inevitably bring about the polarization of income distribution (Hu Daiguang (胡代光), 2004; Yang Shengming (杨圣明), 2005; Zhang Honghai (章洪海) and Gou Juanjuan (苟娟娟), 2005; Zhou Xincheng (周新城), 2006; Zhang Baoping (张保平), 2007; Wang Xiaolu (王小鲁), 2007; Fu Ling (傅玲) and Liu Guibin (刘桂斌), 2008; Xu Xianxiang (徐现祥) and Wang Haigang (王海港), 2008; Zhang Kui (张奎) and Wang Zuxiang (王祖祥), 2009). Some scholars blamed the existence of non-public economy and "the relationship of production and the nature of capitalism" (Tan Zhiling (谭芝灵), 2006). Some scholars thought that "the exploitation" in market competition and China's new non-public economy were the primary cause (Lu Jiarui (卢嘉瑞), 2002). The experience basis of understanding was mainly from official statistical data and empirical surveys. An empirical study discovered that, since the 1990s, China's changing tendency of urban and rural internal income distribution has been the rapid increase of the income share held by the high-income group and unceasing decrease of the income share held by the low-income group (Ma Xiaohe (马晓河), 2003), which has brought about polarization.

The third viewpoint held is that China's high degree of income differential holds the possibility of polarization. Many researchers have carefully raised this argument; some feel the income distribution will level out and is even under control; they do not think that this status means China's income differential has achieved polarization but has the possibility of polarization; most claim that undoing this trend is worth vigilance, and existing differentiation tendencies should be checked or reversed as soon as possible to avoid more serious differentials and polarization (Sun Liping (孙立平), 2003; Li Shi (李实) and Zuo Tenghong (佐腾宏), 2004; Liu Guoguang (刘国光), 2005; Guo Fei (郭飞), 2005; Quan Heng (权衡), 2006; Wang, 2006; Song Shiyun (宋士云), 2007). Some documents used the concept of polarization in the analysis, and studied the change of

income differential according to a polarization index (Hong Xingjian
(洪兴建), and Li Jinchang (李金昌), 2007; Zhang Taoxin (张陶新), 2009),
but in fact did not determine whether polarization has really appeared
because the "polarization" that they said is still just an income differential;
this work also reached a strange conclusion that current income's "polarization degree is actually quite moderate" (Zhang Taoxin, 2009).

The theory basis cited in the first kind of position is questionable,
even though we do not claim whether the Kuznets hypothesis has
become the "principle" of income distribution change confirmed universally by the empirical results. It also seems many of these researchers
have misunderstood Marx and Deng Xiaoping's related discussions.
Truly, Marx's polarization is related to private ownership of the means
of production and is the differentiation of the possession of means of
production; but simultaneously it is also related to the polarization of
income and wealth distribution to form the pattern in which one pole
accumulates wealth, while the other pole accumulates the poverty.[1]
Deng Xiaoping's viewpoint on China's polarization developed over
time. Before the mid-1980s, Deng Xiaoping also understood polarization from the angle of class differentiation. When he adopted a position of reform, he truly believed that China would not present
polarization patterns because of two important principles: first, the
public economy would occupy the principal status, in this way a new
bourgeoisie would not come into being; second, he insisted on the
principle of common prosperity, in this way the pattern of popularization between the rich and poor would not present itself in polarized
income distribution (the CCCPC Party Literature Research Office,
2004). Even if Deng Xiaoping did not restrict polarization in class differentiation, the popularization between the rich and poor was an
important point of focus. After the mid-1980s, Deng Xiaoping's attention obviously shifted; he began to consider the problems caused by
the reality of income polarization in China. In 1993, he said: "we aim
to prevent polarization; but in fact polarization naturally appears"
(CCCPC Party Literature Research Office, 2004, p. 1364). Therefore,
he considered that, in order for China to achieve a better society by the

---

[1] See *Karl Marx and Frederick Engels*, Vol. 1, p. 273 and Vol. 2, p. 259.

end of 20th century, income distribution must be regulated. The transfer of emphasis was not without reason. With China's unceasing reform and opening up, the non-public economy has flourished, and whether the public economy continues to occupy the principal status is more and more debatable.[2] Discussing China's polarization from the angle of income differential should become the main analytical point of view. In fact, the discussion of the international academic circle on polarization has been almost unanimously focused on income polarization (Alderson *et al.*, 2005). Moreover, the income differential cannot simply equal polarization. So long as the existing income differential appeared on the basis of universal enhancement of income level, and so long as there has been a tendency of "rich getting richer, poor getting poorer", claiming that polarization was nonexistent was simplified logic (Wang Jiangui (王检贵), 2000).

Most related documents on this subject have insisted on the second kind of judgment and often directly regard the expansion of income differential as having reached a high degree as direct evidence, which seems to directly regard both as the same. Polarization was certainly the basis of income differential and the high degree can only be considered polarized (Wang Jiangui, 2000). Moreover, most evidence cited by this kind of research, as stated above, referred to absolute differentials of all kinds of income distribution and lacked empirical evidence on the internal

---

[2] According to the statistics of the State-Owned Assets Supervision and Administration in 2006, the real assets of all state-owned and state-owned holding enterprises were about RMB 29 trillion; in the same period, according to the statistics of the State Administration for Industry and Commerce, the registered capital of non-public economic organizations totaled around RMB 16 trillion, and from the sampling survey of all private enterprises by the CPC Central Committee United Front Work Department and the All-China Federation of Industry and Commerce, their real assets were at least twice of the registered capitals. Therefore, in the whole country, the real assets of non-public economy might exceed the public economy. According to the statistics of the National Development and Reform Commission, in 2008, the value added non-public economy accounted for about 60% of GDP (Jiang Guocheng (江国成), 2009). According to the statistics of the National Bureau of Statistics, in 2007, China's ownership structure of employment was that, state-owned units accounted for 8.34%, collective units accounted for 0.93%, and other units and rural households accounted for 90.73%.

structure of differentials and their changing tendencies.[3] Therefore, this viewpoint lacks empirical persuasion.

Most research documents with the third kind of position specially paid attention to the research methods and the sampling survey data. However, the data depended on by this research was acquired early; the latest national sampling survey data was gathered five to six years ago. Considering that China's income distribution differential has been expanding year by year, the current income distribution differentials need to be explained with new data. Moreover, the degree of income differential discovered in this research was actually very high; only because the standards of defining polarization do not have a consensus, their conclusions appeared excessively cautious.

Whether China's income distribution differential has presented a polarization trend is not a theory but an experience. The aggregate indicators of income differential have reached very high levels. For example, the differential between Chinese urban and rural incomes was the first or second largest in the world (Knight and Song, 1999; Eastwood and Lipton, 2004); moreover, according to our task group's survey in 2006, the Gini coefficient of national income distribution in 2005 was almost 0.5 (Li Peilin (李培林) *et al.*, 2008), which was similarly very high internationally (see Table 6.1). In terms of international experiences, this level of overall income differential has provided the conditions for the polarization of income distribution. Some research pointed out that, even if a country's aggregate indicators of income differential do not reach China's level, these countries can be described as polarized. For example, Alderson *et al.* studied the tendency of income differential change for 16 OECD core countries based on the data of the Luxembourg income survey, and the results showed that these countries' income distribution had polarization tendencies (Alderson *et al.*, 2005). But from the data in Table 6.1, in the 30 countries of the OECD, the Gini coefficient of income distribution of

---

[3] Some researches carried on the system study based on empirical data, but its income data was either based on the distribution of payment for labor of various provinces estimated based on the national statistical data (such as, Xu Xianxiang (徐现祥) and Wang Haigang (王海港), 2008) or only involved in few areas but not the whole country (such as Zhang Kui (张奎) and Wang Zuxiang (王祖祥) 2009)).

Table 6.1.   Gini Coefficient Grouping Distribution of Various Countries (Regions) in Recent Years.

	Europe	North America	Latin America	Oceania	Africa	Asia	Total
0.2–0.299	19	0	0	0	0	1	20
0.3–0.399	21	1	0	2	11	17	52
0.4–0.499	2	1	8	0	13	8	32
0.5–0.599	0	1	12	1	5	3	22
0.6 above	0	0	0	0	5	0	5
Total	42	3	20	3	34	29	131
Maximum value	Russia 0.413	Mexico 0.509	Bolivia 0.592	Papua new guinea 0.509	Namibia 0.707	Singapore 0.522	

Note: (1) In the Asian part, excluding Hong Kong, China and Taiwan, China. Hong Kong's Gini coefficient of income distribution in 2007 was 0.533 and Taiwan's Gini coefficient in 2000 was 0.326. (2) In the original data, Mainland China's Gini coefficient was 0.470, which was possibly under-estimated. China had actually entered change phase of 0.5 above. (3) In the table, 13 countries' data came from the 1990s, and 120 countries' data came after the 21st century.

Source: Ordering has been done according to data provided by CIA (2003–2008).

Mexico (0.509 in 2005), the United States (0.45 in 2007), and Turkey (0.436 in 2003) surpassed 0.4.

Therefore, based on international experience as well as the fact that China's Gini coefficient of income differential has approached and even surpassed 0.5, it is well-founded for us to raise the following hypotheses on China's income differential change patterns: based on China's change of income differential patterns until now, there is a clear polarization situation, and this situation is gradually intensifying (Hypothesis 1).

Certainly, we also know that China's income differential degree started to rise after reform and opening up; the massive findings gave this claim confirmation, which was compounded by the Gini coefficient of national income distribution announced by the national department concerned which also rose from 0.288 in 1982 to 0.349 in 1988. However, we must note that, for over 30 years, the effect of different mechanisms was behind change of income differential in China. The reform in the 1980s was in order to arouse people's enthusiasm under the condition that they did not give up a planned economic system, not to establish a market economy system (Chen Guangjin (陈光金), 1996); at that time, the "birdcage theory" ("鸟笼说" *niao long shuo*) prevailed in China and provided a good explanation on overall characteristics of reform at this time. Although the rural Gini coefficient of income distribution experienced a large rise, the urban Gini coefficient actually remained below 0.3 (He Ya (何娅), 2007). Therefore, it is observed that, at this stage, China's Gini coefficient of income distribution surpassed 0.3 because of the sudden appearance of rural household-based contract system reform and rural enterprises, and these reforms and developments contained market principles, but their nature was not of general adoption of market principles as a whole. The years from 1989 to 1991 was a special period for Chinese economic and social development; the characteristic of the period was that the development of the economic domain, except the planned system, was suppressed and even attacked. The differential dropped in this period of time; according to the data announced by the National Bureau of Statistics, China's Gini coefficient was 0.360 in 1989, 0.348 in 1990, and then increased slightly in 1991 to 0.362. It is possible that this official data underestimated the income differential degree at that time. After 1992, it is well known that China entered a reform stage in order to establish a market economy system, and it prominently displayed large-scale restructuring of rural enterprises and state-owned enterprises. Generally speaking, this reform has continued until today; now, China's economy and society has had profound restructuring and reforming. According to the research (Nielsen and Alderson, 1997; Alderson *et al.*, 2005), the OECD core countries' income distribution presented an inverted U curve change because of neoliberalism reform, which started in the late-1970s (certainly there were also other reasons, such as globalization). Considering China's changing patterns of income differential over nearly 20 years, we may raise a second hypothesis: since the late-1980s, China's income differential also had some degree of U curve characteristics and the bottom turning point of this U curve change will approximately align with the time when the restructuring of rural enterprises and state-owned enterprises is completed (Hypothesis 2). This is because these restructurings have had dual influences. At the initial and mid-stages of this restructuring, the differential will drop. For example, the restructuring of rural enterprises broke down original rural community jurisdiction; some distribution and redistribution eliminated the superiority of people in the community of rural enterprises and the differential between rural communities of other areas and the communities with developed rural enterprises was reduced. Once this restructuring was completed, a new opportunity structure and interest structure were formed (Sun Liping (孙立平), 2002). Income distribution would be forced to evolve according to inherent tendencies of expansion and polarization.

Regarding China's future tendencies of income differential, academic circles also have widespread arguments. As stated above, when discussing China's income differential, some scholars unceasingly cite the Kuznets hypothesis (Kuznets, 1955), which influenced the research of international academic circles on income differentials for more than 50 years. These theories either attempt to prove that China's income differential would follow the regular tendency raised in this hypothesis or that it was not applicable in China's changing tendencies of income differential. This hypothesis believed that, under the market economy system, along with the development of industrialization and urbanization, a country's change of income distribution differential presents a tendency that rises to some inflexion first and then drops, which is the so-called inverted U curve tendency of income differential. Based on this tendency judgment, this hypothesis also concluded that (1) in developing countries, the income differential in urban areas is higher than in rural areas; (2) in developing countries, the agricultural sector's differential is smaller than the non-agricultural sector.

Some research has also unceasingly declared that China's changing tendencies of income differential gave the positive confirmation to the inverted U curve hypothesis (Chen Zongsheng (陈宗胜), 2000; Guo Xibao (郭熙保), 2002; Guan Xiaoming (管晓明), 2006), but under market conditions, as China's income differentials change, it seems as if it is too early to think that this hypothesis has been confirmed (Li Shi (李实), 2000; Ding Renzhong (丁任重), Chen Zhizhou (陈志舟) and Gu Wenjun (顾文军), 2003; Wang Xiaolu (王小鲁) and Fan Gang (樊纲), 2005). The aforementioned two assertions of income distribution change on urban and rural areas of developing countries and agricultural and non-agricultural sectors based on the Kuznets hypothesis are worth considering; it has provided us a feasible means and operation hypothesis to examine the Kuznets hypothesis. China is still a developing country, but the marketization of the Chinese economy has achieved a higher level. Therefore, according to the above two Kuznets assertions, we can raise two trend hypotheses: first, with the lapse of time, the income differential of urban areas will become higher than that of rural areas (Hypothesis 3); second, with the lapse of time, the income differential of the agricultural sector will be smaller than the non-agricultural sector (Hypothesis 4). If these two trends really occur, it may be anticipated that, according to the Kuznets hypothesis, China's income distribution differential will reduce along with economic development.

When carrying on disassembly studies on the changes of income distribution differentials of a country internationally, they discovered that the income differential change may attribute to both the income structure change and income's central tendency to change on the whole. It is believed that, in modern society, the inverted U curve hypothesis on income differential change is essentially related to income distribution's structural change (Wan Guanghua (万广华), 2008). Income structural change refers to, under a dual economic structure, a national economic structure that has significantly readjusted, that is, while the traditional sectors gradually wither, the modern sectors gradually expand, and finally the entire economy accomplishes modernization. With unceasing structural readjustment, the structural effects of income differential will also unceasingly attenuate and eventually vanish. As stated above, the reform process has made a great deal of progress in China. Although the change in urban and rural structures lag behind the change of economic structure, the marketability level of employment, ownership structure, and non-socialization of GDP structure all have made significant progress. Regarding China's future tendencies of income differential, we may raise a third hypothesis: with the lapse of time, the structural effects of income distribution differential will attenuate and central effects will strengthen (Hypothesis 5). If this hypothesis is confirmed, China's future income differential changing tendency will conform to the inverted U curve hypothesis.

II. Data and Research Methods

A. *Explanations on research data*

This chapter regards two kinds of data as the analysis basis. The first kind of data is from the CSS by the task group in 2008. This survey used the principles of multistage proportional sampling; our sample covers 28 provinces (excluding Hainan, Tibet and Gansu provinces), in which 135 countries (city, district), 257 townships, 520 villagers' and residents' committees were sampled, ultimately obtaining 7,139 respondents for the questionnaire interview. The survey covered basic information of household population and members' employment status and investigated the households' net incomes and sources of income in 2007. This data has been used as the research basis in this chapter. The second kind of data is from the China Health and Nutrition Survey (CHNS); this survey was jointly implemented by the University of North Carolina and the Chinese Academy of Preventive Medicine.[4] The survey began in 1989, and surveyed, respectively, households' populations, employment, and income in the previous year in 1991, 1993, 1997, 2000, 2004, and 2006. The survey used the method of multi-stage stratified random cluster sampling according to geographical location, economic development levels, public resources, and the health index. It covered eight to nine provinces in eastern, central, and western areas of China.[5] Except select provincial capitals and low-income cities of each province, we sampled four counties at random according to income stratification (high, middle, and low); we then sampled counties, towns, and three villages according to the income stratification in each county, and 20 sample households to represent each village, urban area, and suburb. As compared with the statistical data of

---

[4]The author wishes to thank the joint sponsors, U.S. National Institutes of Health (R01-HD30880, DK056350, and R01-HD38700), Carolina Population Center, and the Chinese Center for Disease Control and Prevention investigators who generously provided the author a seven-year survey data.
[5]The eight provinces surveyed in 1989, 1991, and 1993 are: Liaoning, Jiangsu, Shandong, Henan, Hubei, Hunan, Guangxi, and Guizhou. Heilongjiang province replaced Liaoning in 1996; Liaoning survey was restored after 1999.

the National Bureau of Statistics, the sample households' income level surveyed was equal to the level announced by the National Bureau of Statistics. This study encompassed the data of an eight-year nationwide household income survey from 1988 to 2007.

The task group's household income survey items in the national sampling survey in 2008 included migrant household's income and family-run agricultural operations, the income of non-agricultural operations (operating profit and draw extra dividends etc.), wages (contains wages, income of bonus and allowance on wages as well as retirement income etc.), property income (income for leasing, income of deposit interest), non-wage subsidy income (subsidy income from government and community, income of minimum living security, relief income) as well as other incomes (such as grant income etc.); these incomes all belong to the net income, which had deductions from production operation cost and the expenses of taxation figured in. The income scope defined by CHNS is that of the net income of family-run agricultural operations, income of non-agricultural operations, the family's gross wage income (including wages, bonus as well as all kinds of subsidy on work), gross retirement income, gross subsidy income (government and community's transfer income), and gross income from other sources (including all kinds of property income, grant income etc.). Generally speaking, the income definition of these two kinds of data is the same. The task group's survey differentiated property income from income from other sources, and the CHNS data differentiated retirement pensions from wage income. The CHNS data publicized had been revised according to the household information surveyed as well as the price index in 2006. To conform to this revised data, we processed the sample household income according to consumer price indices of various provinces in 2007.

The issue is that CHNS surveys had a follow-up survey nature; in the meantime, the consistency of data is unquestionable. To be comparable with CHNS survey, GSS•CASS survey needs to have similar interviewee principal character distribution structure of the CHNS survey. In addition, there is the issue of whether cruising data can be the representative of the national situation. Table 6.2 describes interviewees' principal character distribution structures (excluding students in school) from

Table 6.2. Interviewee's Basic Distribution Structure in All Previous Surveys.

		1989	1991	1993	1997	2000	2004	2006	2008
Sex	Man	50.8	50.9	51	51.9	51.7	50.4	50.6	49.8
	Woman	49.2	49.1	49	48.1	48.3	49.6	49.4	50.2
	Sample number	9,325	9,175	8,590	8,780	8,814	7,467	7,065	6,789
Age	Mean value	37.4	38.4	39.4	40.8	42.7	46.6	48.3	45.2
	Standard deviation	14.8	14.7	14.8	14.7	14.8	15	14.7	13.2
	Sample number	9,373	9,103	8,579	8,549	9,156	7,467	7,064	6,789
Educational level (year)	Mean value	7.6	7.7	7.8	9.5	8.5	8.6	9.5	8.5
	Standard deviation	4	3.9	3.8	2.9	3.7	3.8	4.2	4
	Sample number	9,364	9,158	8,577	8,878	9,281	7,459	7,070	6,789
Household registration	Non-agriculture	32.6	30.8	34.1	36.2	37	40.7	40.8	37.1
	Agriculture	67.4	69.2	65.9	63.8	63	59.3	59.2	62.9
	Sample number	9,373	9,178	8,595	8,878	9,248	7,366	6,910	6,789
Employment sector	Agriculture	52.8	55.3	53.9	51.9	48.2	56.4	45.7	47.4
	Non-agriculture	47.2	44.7	46.1	48.1	51.8	43.6	54.3	52.6
	Sample number	8,538	8,529	7,928	8,058	8,316	6,133	5,894	5,244

(Continued)

Table 6.2. (*Continued*)

Nature of non-agricultural employment		1989	1991	1993	1997	2000	2004	2006	2008
	Inside system	45.7	49	42.8	34.8	31.1	31.5	26.6	23.5
	Outside system	54.3	51	54.2	65.2	68.9	68.5	73.4	76.5
	Sample number	3,833	5,368	3,758	4,031	4,466	2,791	3,259	2,477

Note: Unit: %. (1) Sex structure. In the CHNS survey, interviewees' sex distributions in all previous years were approximately the same; men slightly outnumbered women. In our 2008 survey, after comparison, women slightly outnumbered men, but in the two sets of cruising data, interviewees' difference of sex structure was very small, which will not affect related analysis. (2) Age structure. From 1989 to 2008, interviewees' average age assumed an upward trend, which was consistent with China's general trend of aging. Certainly, the cruising data in column 2 does not reflect total population, only the 16 years old and above population; therefore, the average age in the survey does not represent the average age of the total population. In terms of standard deviation of age distribution during survey years, interviewees' internal structure of age distribution was also roughly similar. (3) Educational level. Over the eight years of surveys, interviewees' education levels showed a growth trend as a whole, which had similarly reflected China's general trend of education development. However, interviewees' average education was possibly higher than the average educational level of the 15 years old and above population; for example, it is estimated according to the National Census data in 2000 that the average education level of the 15 years old and above population was 7.11 years in the same year in which the CHNS estimation was 1.4 years higher. Considering this point, the survey results were not excessively bigger than the deviation of the actual average education level for 16 years old and above population. (4) Household registration. On all previous survey results, China's urbanization process was clearly reflected; namely, the proportion of non-agricultural household registration assumed an upward trend as a whole. As compared with the CHNS survey in 2006, in the GSS•CASS 2008 survey, the proportion of non-agricultural household registration dropped 3.6%, possibly because we carried on the general weighting of the data from urban and rural areas, age, and sex. When no weighting is applied, in GSS•CASS survey, the proportion of non-agricultural household registration was 43.1% (sample number was 6,972), which did not deviate from the overall tendency. (5) Employment sector. The general trend was that the proportion of agricultural employment dropped, and non-agricultural employment rose, which was also consistent with national trends. However, as compared with the data announced in the *China Statistical Yearbook*, the proportion of agricultural employment was somewhat lower, and then began to rise. If part-time personnel discovered in the survey are completely comprised in the non-agricultural employment sector, this kind of difference can be very small. Generally speaking, the two sets of data are also comparable in this aspect. (6) Non-agricultural employment. In the CHNS survey, the general trend was that the proportion of employment "inside the system" dropped unceasingly, whereas those "outside the system" rose unceasingly. The GSS•CASS survey continued the trends in the CHNS survey; we believed that unifying the two sources of data for analysis was feasible.

Through the summary of the above analyses, it is believed that, first, unifying CHNS cruising data with GSS•CASS cruising data to analyze the income distribution trends from 1989 to 2007 does not have distinct barriers for interviewees' principal character distribution and structural difference. As compared with the official statistics provided in the *China Statistical Yearbook*, the cruising data used here is roughly similar to the total population's related principal character structure; even if both have some differences in the detailed data, it is still basically consistent with total population's changing trends related to principal character structure. Therefore, we may unify these two sets of data to use.

the perspectives of sex, age, educational level, household registration, employment, and employment sector (proportion of few part-time personnel was divided equally to agricultural sector and non-agricultural sector).

B. *Explanations on research methods*

(1) *Methods on studying the income differential's changing pattern*

This section provides quantitative analysis of China's income differential's changing pattern for 20 years. We first calculated the measuring targets of overall income differential during the 20 years examined, in which the Gini coefficient was utilized most widely. The Gini coefficient has many computing modes, and the results from different methods have slight differences. We calculated the Gini coefficient (expressed by '*G*') with the following mathematical equation based on the Lorenz curve:

$$G = \frac{1}{2n^2 \mu} \left(\sum_{i=1}^{n} \sum_{j=1}^{n} \left| x_i - x_j \right| \right). \tag{1}$$

In the equation, n is the sample number, μ is the sample mean, and x_i is the sample observed value. Chen Zongsheng ((陈宗胜), 1991) once thought that an important standard to judge whether a country's income differential presented polarization was the Gini coefficient of income distribution and its changing trend. He believed that, regarding private-owned economy, if the Gini coefficient reached 0.5 and remained at that level (for perhaps 10 years), polarization would occur. China regards the public-owned economy as the main body, and the Gini coefficient standard should be lower than 0.5—Zongsheng advocated a maximum level of 0.43. Other than the Gini coefficient, there were also other certain targets to measure income differential; according to Wan Guanghua (2008) who discussed the nature of various targets, three targets from the generalized entropy level were a measure as the possibly as good Gini coefficient. The generalized entropy's mathematical expression is as follows:

$$GE = \frac{1}{\alpha(1-\alpha)}\left[\sum_{i=1}^{n}\frac{1}{n}\left(1-\frac{y_i}{\mu}\right)^{\alpha}\right].$$

In the equation, y_i is the income level's observed value, μ is the average income, n is the sample size, and α is a constant that represents the differential aversion degree. When its value is 0, the GE level expresses full aversion differential; at this time the generalized entropy index is the so-called Theil L index (meaning logarithm deviation). If the α value is 1, the generalized entropy index is Theil T index (i.e., usually called the Theil index). If α value is 2, which represents a more tolerant attitude to income differential, the generalized entropy index is called a Theil V index. L and T value scopes are [0, 1], and V value scope is [2, ∞]. Because V index's value scope does not have the upper limit, it is difficult to make judgment of a relative degree according to it; therefore, the following analyses do not consider this index. L and T indices' equations are respectively:

$$GE(0) = \frac{1}{n}\sum_{i=1}^{n}\log\frac{\mu}{y_i} \; ; \; GE(1) = \frac{1}{n}\sum_{i=1}^{n}\frac{y_i}{\mu}\log\frac{y_i}{\mu}. \qquad (2)$$

The Theil index and Gini coefficient have a complementary relationship. The Gini coefficient is particularly sensitive to changes at the middle-income level, whereas the Theil T index is very sensitive to a change in upper income level, and the Theil L index is quite sensitive to the change at the bottom income levels; therefore, these values are often used simultaneously.[6]

These indices are insufficient to comprehensively judge the structural features of income differential. Therefore, some scholars (Li Shi (李实),

---

[6] Some researchers also use Atkinson index. But the index is one-to-one monotone conversion relation with GE index, so once the GE index is available, it is unnecessary to calculate Atkinson index (Wan Guanghua, 2008).

Zhao Renwei (赵人伟) and Zhang Ping (张平), 1998) advocated that the judgment must be made according to average income change trends between the highest and lowest-income groups, as well as the changing trend of the ratio between their average income and the median income. Following this reasoning, if the average income of the highest-income groups grows, and those of the lowest-income group drop, or the ratio the between former's average income and the median income rises, while the ratio between the latter's average income and the median income drops, it may be thought that the income differential presents a polarization pattern. The former is called "absolute standard", and the latter is "relative standard". These two standards' significance is clear but is also deficient in some ways. For example, the average income between the highest and lowest-income groups can possibly grow, but the former's growth is quicker; the share of the highest-income group in gross income also rises quicker. The latter possibly rises slowly so that the share of the lowest-income group actually drops; in this case, generally speaking, the change of income differential still has the nature of polarization. Therefore, as a supplement, here we raise a "share standard", namely a respective change of the income shares of the highest and lowest-income groups. If they change deviation direction toward each other, it is observed that there is a polarization trend.

We should point out that the measurement of income differential and change thereof was restricted in the comparison of overall differential with the income changes of the highest and lowest-income groups. This analysis did not yet address the internal structural features of income differential changes. Therefore, one new analysis method was introduced. Handcock and Morris (1999) provided one method to distinguish income distribution's patterns of change. This method was based on "relative distribution", which was defined as the ratio between the sample household proportion of some income groups in benchmark years and the household proportion of this income group in reference years, as well as the grouping mode. The sample households of the benchmark years are first divided into 10 groups (or 5 groups), and then, to eliminate the influence of decile changes, the ratio between the median incomes of benchmark and reference years is regarded as the weight to adjust the income for a reference year. Finally, the sample households of reference years are divided into

10 groups according to the deciles of the benchmark year, if the proportion of some group in the sample households of reference year rises or falls, the relative distribution will also rise or drop. If there is no change, the entire distribution structure will be smooth. Income distribution's changing patterns in this period may be judged by these figures. This method allows analysis of polarization from the angle of household grouping distribution changes and is an important supplement to purely study polarization from the angle of income differential.

It is necessary to further measure the degree of polarization. Academic circles have raised many targets to measure the degree of polarization such as *W* index and *ER* polarization index. Some scholars have pointed out that, regarding the endogenic group data, it is possible to analyze the degree of polarization with the *W* index. Moreover, research indicated that the *W* index was a special instance of the *ER* index when grouping according to the median. *W* index was raised by Wolfson (1994); he gave the following equation to measure the polarization based on the polarization curve concept:

$$W = \frac{2(2T - G)}{m/\mu}.$$ (3)

In the equation, m and μ are respectively all interviewees' income median and arithmetic mean, G is the Gini coefficient, T is the difference between the 50% lowest income population's share and its income share, namely $T = 0.5 - L$ (0.5), L (0.5) expresses the income share of the 50% of the lowest income interviewees.

It is insufficient to merely understand the degree of polarization on the basis of median groupings; therefore, we also need to understand the contribution of each group in terms of polarization. Handcock and Morris constructed a "median income relative polarization index" (MRP) on the basis of the median relative distribution method, and *MRP* index's mathematical expression is as follows:

$$MRP_t(Q) = \frac{4}{Q-2} \sum_{i=1}^{Q} \left| \frac{2i-1}{2Q} - \frac{1}{2} \right| \times g_t(i) - \frac{Q}{Q-2}.$$ (4)

In this equation, $g_t(i)$ is the relative distribution; after adjustment by median, its income falls into the ratio between the household proportion in t year between a pair of income tangent points and the household proportion of corresponding income groups in a benchmark year, $i = 1$, $2, \ldots, Q$. The range of MRP values is $[-1, 1]$. When some income group's household distribution in t year does not relatively change to corresponding distribution in the benchmark year, *MRP* is 0; when it is positive value, *MRP* expresses its relative polarization, and when there is a negative value, it expresses its convergence of income distribution. The *MRP* polarization index may be disassembled into the contribution of distribution changes of median above and below. The relative distribution polarization index of median below (LRP) and the relative polarization index of median above (URP) may be calculated according to following equation:

$$LRP_t / URP_t(Q) = \frac{8}{Q-2} \sum_{i}^{Q/2} \left| \frac{2i-1}{2Q} - \frac{1}{2} \right| \times g_t(i) - \frac{Q}{Q-2}, \qquad (5a)$$

$$MRP_t = (LRP_t + URP_t)/2. \qquad (5b)$$

In Equation (5a), regarding the relative distribution polarization index of median below, $i = 1, 2, 3, 4, 5$; regarding relative distribution polarization index of median above, $i = 6, 7, 8, 9, 10$. It should be noted that MRP index is quite sensitive to the relative distribution at both sides of grouping distribution because its equation is entrusted with the maximum weight to the relative distribution at both sides; in this way, the MRP index can well reflect the changes of distribution at both sides of the income spectrum.

(2) *Main methods to study the future change of income differential*

Regarding China's future changes of income differential, this chapter raised three operation hypotheses based on the Kuznets hypothesis. Regarding Hypotheses 3 and 4, the proving method was the income differential disassembly based on Theil index, namely they were respectively grouped by city–countryside and agriculture–non-agriculture groups. When grouping by agriculture–non-agriculture, CHNS data provided annual income of employed people in two sectors every survey year. As for the task group's cruising data in 2008, the related data need to be obtained through estimation, and the method of estimation was analyzed as follows. The targets to measure the income differential of each group also incorporate the Gini coefficient and Theil *T* index.

The method to evaluate Hypothesis 5 is to disassemble the time variation of income differential measured by Gini coefficient (Wan Guanghua, 2008). The logic disassembly analysis then uses sub-item disassembly results based on the annual Gini coefficient; to obtain the Gini coefficient change in different years, the sub-item income share change and the sub-item income concentration ratio change, and to disassemble the Gini coefficient change into the sub-item income share change, the sub-item income concentration ratio change as well as the contribution of the combined action of these two changes. The sub-item income share change was considered as the result of economic structure change; therefore, its contribution to the differential change was the structural effect of income differential change; but the change of sub-item income concentration ratio had reflected the concentricity of each income; thus, it is referred to as the income differential change concentration effect. The Gini coefficient change may be disassembled according to the following equation:

$$\Delta G = \sum_{i=1}^{K} C_{it} \times \Delta S_i + \sum_{i=1}^{K} S_{it} \times \Delta C_i + \sum_{i=1}^{K} \Delta C_i \times \Delta S_i. \qquad (6)$$

In this equation, ΔG is the Gini coefficient's change value, C_{it} is the concentration ratio of i (income) in t year; ΔC_i is change value of i (income), or the concentration ratio; S_{it} is the share of i items of income in the gross income of t year; and ΔS_i is the change value of i in income share. The first item at right hand side of Equation (6) is structural effect, the second item is the concentration effect, and the third item is the common effect of both.

III. Pattern of Change in Urban and Rural Income Differential for 20 Years

A. *Change of differential degree*

We first study basic trends of change of all families' per capita income differential, and detailed computing results are shown in Table 6.3. From Table 6.3, we may see that the average income level has assumed a growing trend, but the distribution differential degree is also increasing; for example, the standard deviation increased obviously every year except 1990, and the deviation between the mean value and the median was also increasing. In brief, the later the year, the higher was the income distribution differential degree. This without a doubt would lead to the expansion of the differential degree of income distribution year by year. The defective index of income distribution fluctuated before the mid-1990s, but rose absolutely after 1999.

The changes of the four indices to measure the differential were also similar; generally speaking, 1996 was a turning point. Before this, the

Table 6.3. Chinese Families' Per Capita Income Distribution Differentials from 1988 to 2007.

	Mean value	Median	Standard deviation	Defective index[a]	L index[b]	T index[b]	Gini coefficient	Sample number
1988	1060.3	892.8	1068	9.9	0.1398	0.1287	0.3990	3,743
1990	1081.8	907.6	816	8.6	0.1222	0.1053	0.3797	3,586
1992	1529.2	1164.7	1376.9	11	0.1017	0.2145	0.4260	3,410
1996	3137.2	2525	2690.6	10.2	0.1418	0.1237	0.4091	3,805
1999	3953.5	2999.6	4247.7	15	0.1841	0.1628	0.4589	4,300
2003	5608.2	3802.9	6081.6	18.8	0.2082	0.1805	0.4943	4,318
2005	6743.6	4306.5	9402.2	21.8	0.2363	0.2179	0.5225	4,359
2007	8237.4	4774	30697	23	0.2465	0.2445	0.5384[c]	6,986

Note: [a] denotes the ratio between income shares of 20% of highest-income people and 20% of lowest-income people.

[b] When calculating these Theil indices, households with income that was 0 were deleted (because its logarithm value cannot be calculated); in addition, an extreme in data in 2007 was deleted, namely RMB 2,362,000, as it would have unreasonable enormous influence on *T* index.

[c] When calculating, the extreme value of RMB 2,362,000 was deleted.

changes of the T index and of the Gini coefficient fluctuated, and the L index assumed a declining trend. Thereafter, the four indexes steadily rose and ultimately reached a very high level by 2007. Reviewing China's course of reform, 1996 was truly an important year; through marketization reform starting in 1992, almost all township collective enterprises were restructured. Some township collective enterprises went bankrupt, while the majority became privatized. The overwhelming majority of urban collective enterprises and of middle and small-scale state-owned enterprises also had similar restructuring. Such large-scale enterprise restructuring events inevitably had a major impact on China's income distribution, and Table 6.3 reflects this kind of impact. Hence, it is difficult for some scholars (e.g., Chen Zhiwu, 2006) to reach a conclusion about marketization and privatization movements as a function to reduce the income differential.

B. *Chinese families' structural features of per capita income differential change for 20 years*

We studied the structural features of urban and rural residents' income differential changes for 20 years, namely through analysis of the highest and lowest-income groups' income distribution changes. We looked into whether the income differential had a polarization trend. Here, we divided households sampled into 10 groups according to a general method, and related analysis results are shown in Table 6.4. Based on Table 6.4, the following results may be obtained.

After comparing the two income groups' change of per capita income mean over the 20 years investigated, we may see that the two income groups' average income mean was growing as a whole; therefore, even if there is the income differential polarization trend, it is not a vicious polarization in which high-income groups' income increases, but low-income groups' income decreases. It should be noted that the lowest-income group's per capita income mean growth range was obviously smaller than the highest-income group; moreover, the former's stability was also much worse. This result indicated that the lowest-income group's per capita income mean growth cannot always catch up with the highest-income group.

After comparing the position changes of the two income groups' per capita income mean relative to all samples' per capita income median,

Table 6.4. Chinese Families' Structural Feature of Per Capita Income Differential Change from 1988 to 2007.

	10% of lowest-income group				10% of highest-income group				Ratio of income share[c]
	Average income (RMB)	Annual growth rate (%)[a]	Mean/median[b]	Income share (%)	Average income (RMB)	Annual growth rate (%)[a]	Mean/median[b]	Income share (%)	
1988	147.5	—	0.1652	1.39	2952.9	—	3.3075	27.83	20
1990	172.5	8.17	0.1902	1.60	2815.5	−2.35	3.1021	25.98	16.3
1992	203.4	8.55	0.1746	1.33	4509.1	26.55	3.8715	29.49	22.2
1996	417.7	19.71	0.1654	1.33	8935.9	18.65	3.5390	28.45	21.3
1999	349.3	−5.78	0.1164	0.88	12833.2	12.82	4.2783	32.46	36.7
2003	408.5	3.99	0.1074	0.73	19674.2	11.27	5.1735	35.02	48.1
2005	429.1	2.49	0.0996	0.63	25462.8	13.76	5.9126	37.68	59.4
2007	579.6	16.22	0.1214	0.70	35302.7	17.75	7.3948	42.82	60.8

Note: [a] Here the formula of annual growth rate used is $\left(\sqrt[N]{I_n/I_1}-1\right)\times100\%$; in the equation, I_1 is the average income of reference year, and N is number of years. It is calculated according to the equation, in 20 years, 10% of lowest-income group's average income grew 7.47% every year, and 10% of highest-income group's average income grew 13.95% every year. Moreover, because the cruising data was made through supplemental processing, here the income was comparable.
[b] denotes per capita income median as 1.
[c] denotes 10% of lowest-income group's income share as 1.

we may see that, for the lowest-income group, this position dropped steadily from 1990 to 2005 and went up in 2007. For the highest-income group, the relative income position was largely higher than the lowest-income group throughout; this income group's relative position had fluctuation before 1996, while after 1996, its relative income position always rose. Thereby we may judge that, in most of the 20 years investigated, the lowest-income group's relative income position trend was opposite to that of the highest-income group, which represents an important attribute for the income differential to display trends of polarization.

The lowest-income group's income share dropped steadily from 1990 to 2005, and rose slightly in 2007, which did not influence the highest-income group's share to rise with an unprecedented scope. The highest-income group's income share experienced fluctuation before 1996, while the lowest-income group's income share dropped; this fluctuation should have coincided with the fluctuation of income share of other income groups as well. After 1996, the highest-income group's income share rose steadily, basically raising 1% per year. This change also similarly indicated that, in most years of the 20 years investigated, the highest-income group's income share presented a negative direction change trend toward the lowest-income group. Certainly, because the lowest-income group's range of income decline was smaller than 1% per year, the share of certain income groups in the middle position would also drop. Finally, the ratio between the highest- and lowest-income groups' income shares fluctuated before 1996 and then rose rapidly after 1996.

In summary of the above results, it is observed that, in the 20 years investigated, Chinese urban and rural residents' income differential change had the feature of polarization to a great degree.

C. *Relative distribution change patterns of households/ population grouped by income*

To further observe the internal structural features of the income differential's changing pattern, we adjusted and regrouped the subsequent seven-year's interviewee households' per capita income using Handcock and

Morris' analysis methods of "relative income" distribution based on the interviewee households' median and decile of per capita income distribution in 1988 and obtained each group's distribution change pattern. Figure 6.1 is the analytical result, in which the left figure is each group's proportion change pattern calculated after the household grouping, and the right figure is each group's population proportion change pattern calculated after the household grouping.

To the left of Figure 6.1, in 1996 and before, the income differential change was basically summarized as the increase of highest-income group's relative distribution, and the reduction of lowest-income group's relative distribution. After 1996, the highest-income group's relative distribution unceasingly maintained higher proportions. Simultaneously, the lowest-income group's relative distribution also had an upward trend, but every middle group's proportion experienced a downward trend. In other words, the interviewee households' relative distribution trend moved toward both sides.

In the right chart of Figure 6.1, the general trend is roughly the same as the left one, but it is noteworthy that, in 1988 survey, the relative distribution of the lowest-income group's population approximately presented the shape of a double peak, the population proportion of Group 1 (lowest-income group), Group 6, and Group 9 were relatively low, and that of Group 4, Group 8, and Group 10 (highest-income group) was relatively high, which indicated the income differential did not really experience polarization at this time. In 1992 and 1996, each group of the population's

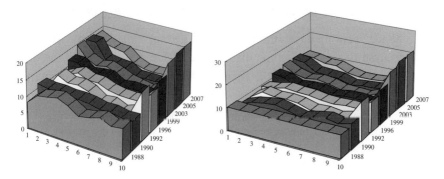

Figure 6.1.   Ten Groups' "Relative Income" Distribution Change in Base Period of 1988.

relative distribution started to have a polarization trend. The highest-income group's population proportion rose obviously, while the low-income groups also went up, whereas the middle income group's population proportion went down. In the subsequent four years, the grouping population's relative distribution more obviously moved toward both sides, every middle group's relative distribution of population obviously presented concavity; relative population distribution of several income groups nearby the highest-income group more obviously displayed this concavity, and this represented an obvious polarization trend.

Comparing the left figure with the right one in Figure 6.1, we may see that, when grouping by household, the lowest-income group's relative distribution did not increase substantially; the proportion was less than 13% at most and grew by less than 30% of this proportion in the benchmark year. The highest-income group's proportion reached 21.5% at most, which was more than 15% greater than the proportion in the benchmark year, it is obvious these figures leaned toward the highest-income group in terms of structural patterns of polarization. When considering each group's population, the difference of relative population distribution at the two poles was smaller, the lowest-income group's population proportion was nearly 15% at most, which grew 88% over the proportion in the benchmark year; the highest-income group's population proportion was 17.4% at most, which grew 87% over the benchmark year. Obviously, after adding the factor of household population, the polarization degree was more remarkable.[7]

D. *Polarization index of income distribution differential*

The above sections have straightened out certain indices to measure the polarization degree of income distribution differential based on the data obtained; here we mainly use *W* and MRP indices, and the computing

---

[7] It should be noted that Handcock and Morris only made a suggestion to investigate the changes of relative distribution by household grouping, and we spread this method, namely analyzed every group's changes of the relative distribution of the family population after grouping by household. Results show that this spread was of great significance, especially in China, as a unit of living, the family overall influences every family member, and therefore such spread is necessary.

results are shown in Table 6.5. Generally speaking, the change of the polarization indices had similar features with the aforementioned changes of income differential, with a turning point in 1996. Before this, the polarization indices fluctuated, and presented a tendency of initial increase and eventual decline; afterward, every distribution polarization index went up.

The polarization level of income distribution measured by the W index was higher. This index mainly took into account the households at median income on the premise of considering the Gini coefficient, and these did not consider the households at the median income that did not belong to the 10% highest-income group. This possibly exaggerated the polarization degree of income distribution. The MRP index compensated for this flaw well because it considered relative distribution change within each grouping. Although the W index was bigger in 2007 compared to 1988, its rate of increase was 69.7%; the MRP index's rate of increase was obviously bigger: without considering the household population, the MRP in 2007 rose approximately 1.8 times over its level in 1992 (and approximately two times the 1992 level in 2005). When considering the household population, the MRP in 2007 rose approximately 4.3 times over the level of

Table 6.5. Urban and Rural Residents' Polarization Indexes of Income Distribution from 1988 to 2007.

	W	MRP when without considering household population			MRP when considering household population		
		LRP	URP	MRP	LRP	URP	MRP
1988	0.3530	—	—	—	—	—	—
1990	0.3892	−0.0555	0.0490	−0.0033	0.1291	−0.0363	0.0464
1992	0.4186	−0.0280	0.1750	0.0735	0.0329	0.1529	0.0929
1996	0.3819	−0.0260	0.0860	0.0300	0.0308	0.0737	0.0522
1999	0.4241	0.0775	0.1415	0.1095	0.1736	0.1065	0.1401
2003	0.5014	0.0905	0.2690	0.1798	0.2898	0.1862	0.2380
2005	0.5766	0.1250	0.3135	0.2193	0.3570	0.1932	0.2751
2007	0.5993	0.0950	0.3120	0.2035	0.3091	0.1809	0.2450

1990 (rose 4.9 times in 2005). Also, without considering the household population, MRP in 1992 was even convergent relative to 1988; namely it was illustrating an anti-polarization trend.

The MRP index also published more information. First, without considering the household population, the LRP index had a negative value in three years, which represented a reduction of polarization in this period. In other years, the LRP index was also smaller than the URP, and thus the URP had a bigger contribution to MRP. When considering the household population scale, the LRP index was bigger than the URP in all years, which indicated that LRP made a bigger contribution to MRP from the angle of the household population. The position of the bigger proportion of population in income distribution functions moved down and from this angle, China's situation of income distribution differential was more serious.

In summary, considering the changing patterns of different polarization indices as well their structural features, the income distribution differential truly experienced a polarization trend; particularly from the MRP index, the income differential changed from convergence to massive polarization.

IV. Possible Change of Income Distribution Differential in the Future

A. *Urban and rural internal differentials: whether the urban internal differential degree is higher*

The analysis method to evaluate Chinese rural and urban internal income differentials in the 20 years investigated is simple, that is, respectively calculating their Theil indices and Gini coefficients. The computing results are shown in Table 6.6. We may see that, first, whether in countryside or city, the common trend of income differential change is basically the same as overall differential change trends, namely regarding 1996 as a turning point. Previously, rural and urban internal differentials fluctuated; thereafter, they went up in all ways, as did the *L* index, *T* index, and Gini coefficient, especially.

The *L* index, *T* index, and Gini coefficient to measure the rural differential were higher than corresponding indices of urban differentials.

Table 6.6.   Changes of Rural and Urban Internal Differentials.

	Rural area			Urban area		
	L index	*T* index	Gini coefficient	*L* index	*T* index	Gini coefficient
1988	0.1545	0.1411	0.4253	0.0804	0.0889	0.3112
1990	0.1320	0.1190	0.4012	0.0783	0.0670	0.2988
1992	0.1553	0.1345	0.4290	0.1258	0.1107	0.3783
1996	0.1383	0.1239	0.4112	0.1255	0.1045	0.3708
1999	0.1773	0.1575	0.4541	0.1549	0.1368	0.4148
2003	0.1932	0.1704	0.4828	0.1878	0.1498	0.4558
2005	0.2214	0.2064	0.5145	0.2151	0.1929	0.4840
2007	0.2234	0.2261	0.5135	0.2169	0.2141	0.4883

Rural and urban differentials were slightly lower than the overall differential, but the differential was not big; particularly after 1996, these three indices changed basically in parallel and rural differentials approached urban differentials by 2007. Figure 6.2 presents this change trend graphically.

In brief, although we only have eight years of cruising data to analyze, we are confident in the evaluation of the 20 years investigated. Generally speaking, the urban differential was not bigger than rural differential. Therefore, above-mentioned Hypothesis 3 cannot be supported.

B. *Sector internal differential: which differential is bigger in agricultural and non-agricultural sectors?*

The CHNS survey obtained information on each employed person's employment sector and net income over the year prior to the survey, which may be used to analyze agricultural and non-agricultural sectors' income differential changes (excluding part-time personnel). In the 2008 survey, our task group enquired about the non-agricultural employed people's income or operating income obtained in the month prior to the survey; information on agricultural workers' income data was lacking, however. According to the real growth rate of rural household operating income in

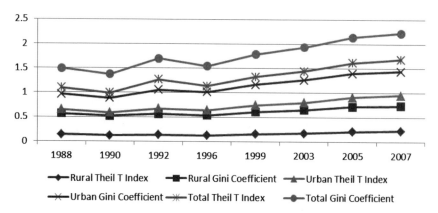

Figure 6.2. Changes of Theil T Index and Gini Coefficient of Urban and Rural Interviewee Households' Income Distribution from 1998 to 2007.

various provinces in 2008, as well as rural households' per capita agricultural operating income in 2007 obtained in the survey, we estimated agricultural employed people's monthly income in 2008, and then we estimated their income value in 2008 according to urban and rural consumer price indices of various provinces in 2007 relative to those of 2006; at the same time, according to urban consumer price indices of various provinces in 2008 relative to those of 2006, we inferred non-agricultural employed people's income in the month before the survey in 2008, thus obtaining agricultural and non-agricultural employed people's annual income distribution in 2008, which may roughly compare with CHNS cruising data. Table 6.7 shows the reflected changes of employed people's income differential in agricultural and non-agricultural sectors over the 20 years investigated. Through analysis of these trends, following conclusions may be drawn.

In the agricultural sector, the general trend also regarded 1996 as a turning point, the differential before this fluctuated with an overall downward trend. After 1996, the differential went upward in fluctuation, which presented a kind of mild U curve shape. Because the L index was bigger than the T index, in the most survey years, the agricultural sector's income distribution mostly gravitated toward the lower end. In terms of the Gini

Table 6.7.   Within-Sector Income Differential Changes.

	Agricultural sector			Non-agricultural sector		
	L index	*T* index	Gini coefficient	*L* index	*T* index	Gini coefficient
1988	0.2406	0.2050	0.5801	0.1471	0.2222	0.4552
1990	0.2226	0.2032	0.5623	0.0871	0.0920	0.4405
1992	0.2480	0.2094	0.5580	0.1185	0.1356	0.3912
1996	0.2085	0.1817	0.5001	0.0978	0.1119	0.3760
1999	0.2358	0.1991	0.4868	0.1141	0.1268	0.3656
2003	0.3065	0.2559	0.5201	0.1299	0.1290	0.3914
2005	0.3106	0.2547	0.5004	0.1674	0.1751	0.3292
2008	0.2875	0.3089	0.5131	0.1612	0.2093	0.4334

coefficient's change, there was a downward trend in the higher levels, in which there was certainly fluctuation (see Figure 6.3a).

In the non-agricultural sector, changes of the two Theil indices presented U curves with a flat bottom. The degree of concavity was bigger than the agricultural sector's corresponding change and its turning point was also in 1996 (see Figure 6.3b). Simultaneously, the Theil *L* index was generally smaller than Theil *T* index, which indicated that the non-agricultural sector's income distribution mostly gravitated toward the upper end. The Gini coefficient change's trend was roughly the same, but the turning point was postponed. Through analysis of the statistical nature of these indices, it is observed that, in the middle period of time within 20 years, the non-agricultural sector's income distribution had relatively bigger densities in the middle section, but the density of distribution was bigger at the upper end before and after this.

However, agricultural and non-agricultural sectors' internal income differentials can change; an invariable trend is that the agricultural sector's internal differential is throughout bigger than the non-agricultural sector. For example, the agricultural sector's Gini coefficient was obviously higher than the non-agricultural sector's Gini coefficient, and the difference was 15.5% at lowest and 34.2% at highest, with an average difference of 24.7%.

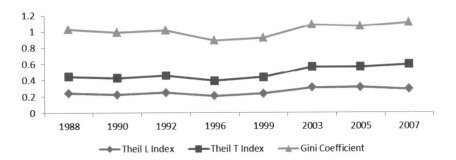

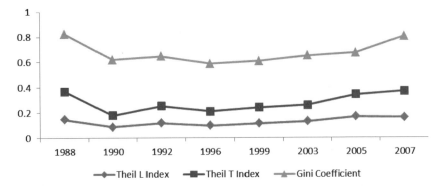

Figure 6.3.   (a) Agricultural Sector's Differential Changes. (b) Non-agricultural Sector's Differential Changes.

*L*指数 (*L zhi shu*): *L* index; *T*指数 (*T zhi shu*): *T* index; 基尼系数 (*ji Ni xi shu*): Gini coefficient.

In summary, whether in the agricultural or non-agricultural sector, there was no inversed U curve trend in the income differential changes. The agricultural sector's differential was throughout higher than the non-agricultural sector, and there was not a stable sign of the former closing in on the latter. Therefore, the aforementioned Hypothesis 4 was not supported.

C. *Structural effect and centralized effect: Which is more prominent?*

The influence of sub-item income differential to the gross income differential, as for its nature, may be divided into three parts: the structural effect, the centralized effect, and the common effect. According to the Kuznets hypothesis, along with economic and social marketization and industrialization development, the structural effect will weaken gradually, and the centralized effect will strengthen gradually. The centralized effect's function enhancement does not mean simply that the income is more centralized. According to the logic of the Kuznets hypothesis, the enhancement of marketization and industrialization levels first means the reduction of structural effects, and because the dual economic structure of developing countries is eradicated in this process, the income differential brought by the structural reforming process will drop to a threshold level, but the income centralization degree will rise, thus, forming another kind of impelling force of the income distribution differential. Along with the further development of marketability and industrialization, the income centralization degree will also drop, thus, finally urging income distribution to evolve toward convergence. Therefore, if these changes exist in a country's trend of income distribution, it may be anticipated that, according to Kuznets hypotheses, this country's income distribution differential will experience an inverted U curve change. According to such principles, we carried on the disassembly analysis of the Gini coefficient change to the cruising data using the aforementioned Equation (6), and obtained the results in Table 6.8. It would be noted that, in Table 6.8, every annual Gini coefficient change is relative to the previous one.

In Table 6.8, over the seven years of surveys, except 1992 and 2003, the function of the structural effect of the other five years to the Gini coefficient change was largely bigger than the function of the centralized effect, if considering the participation of the structural effect in the common effect, this kind of relation would be highlighted. In brief, in the majority of the seven survey years, the structural effect was bigger than the centralized effect.

Figure 6.4 more clearly and intuitively indicated that the contributions of two kinds of effects were basically reversed changes. Particularly after 1996, it was observed that the contribution rate of the two kinds of effects displayed violent ups and downs, which indicated that China's formation mechanism of income distribution differentials were undergoing a period of rapid change. But at the same time, the Gini coefficient change in the majority of survey years mainly originated from the structural effect,

Table 6.8. Disassembly Analysis of Gini Coefficient Change Based on Subitem Income.

	Structural effect		Centralized effect		Common effect			Coefficient change amount[a]
	Contribution amount	Contribution rate	Contribution amount	Contribution rate	Contribution amount	Contribution rate	Contribution rate Total	
1990	-0.0047	-16.9	-0.0184	-66.2	-0.0046	-16.5	-100	-0.0278
1992	0.0071	17.1	0.0370	88.9	-0.0024	-5.8	100	0.0416
1996	0.0043	19.5	-0.0246	-111.8	-0.0017	-7.7	-100	-0.0220
1999	0.0440	57.4	0.0202	26.4	0.0124	16.2	100	0.0766
2003	-0.0217	-40.9	0.0660	124.5	0.0087	16.4	100	0.0530
2005	0.0234	80.1	0.0052	17.8	0.0006	2.1	100	0.0292
2007	0.0323	185.6	-0.0325	-186.8	0.0176	101.2	100	0.0174

Note: [a]As compared with Table 6.7, in this table, Gini coefficient change in various years has little difference possibly because of the rounding process occurred repeatedly in calculation. Our goal, above all, is to analyze the change trend of three kinds of effects, but not these differences.

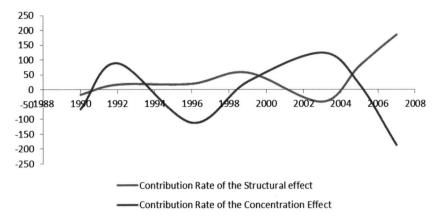

Figure 6.4.   The Changes of the Structural and Concentration Effects of Gini Coefficient.

which indicated that it is highly unlikely for the influence of centralized effects to steadily approach and even surpass the structural effect. In this way, obviously the aforementioned Hypothesis 5 also cannot be supported by the empirical data.

V. A Brief Conclusion

Discovering the degree of income distribution differential is not our main purpose, but is only a basis for further analysis. It is important to research what the nature of bigger differentials truly means, namely, whether there is a polarization trend. According to the existing theory arguments and the remarkably different experiential findings, our hypothesis is that in the 20 years investigated, there was a polarization trend in China's income differential pattern changes (Hypothesis 1). Simultaneously, we also raised a hypothesis on the possible U curve changes (Hypothesis 2). To test Hypothesis 1, we made a multifaceted dissection of the cruising data with many kinds of analysis tools; particularly we thoroughly analyzed China's internal structural features of income differentials and relative distribution changes and calculated the polarization index mainly according to the relative distribution model. We also made a spread of the relative distribution model, namely not only to make the fractional analysis of the households surveyed but also to further consider each household's population scale factor. Our hypothesis was supported by empirical data to a great degree.

China's income differential has grown to a high degree, but how will this differential change in the future? This is an issue of universal concern. Until now, the Kuznets hypothesis was thought to be the soundest theoretical model to forecast the changing trend of income differential. As a theoretical forecasting model, the Kuznets hypothesis involves certain important conditions, and whether these conditions are met becomes a key factor for forecasting the future income differential trends according to this hypothesis; academic circles have developed many theories of the medium-range nature of these conditions. For developing countries, the relative variable of differential between urban and rural societies and between agricultural and non-agricultural sectors, as well as the relative variable of integrated and structural effects to influence the income differential all become criteria for evaluation.

Embarking on such logic and considering that China is not just a developing country, the marketization degree has achieved a higher level, and the economic ownership structure has also undergone tremendous changes; rural labor has entered non-agricultural domains of work and has entered cities to work in staggering numbers; and the economic and social structures have seen profound reform along with this trend. We also raised three related hypotheses: first, as time passes, the urban income differential will be higher than rural area (Hypothesis 3); second, as time passes, the agricultural sector's income differential will be smaller than that of the non-agricultural sector (Hypothesis 4); third, as time passes, the structural effect to cause income distribution differentials will become weaker, and the centralized effect will become stronger (Hypothesis 5). However, the results of our analysis did not support these hypotheses; on the contrary, we saw that the rural income differential was always higher than in urban areas, the agricultural sector's income differential was always higher than non-agricultural sector, and the structural effect on income differential was higher than the centralized effect in the majority of the years surveyed. At present, the data prominently presents the opposite trends. It is difficult to align this data with Kuznets hypothesis.

In the process of testing the above hypotheses, the related analysis results had made an indirect test of Hypothesis 2. Certainly, it seems that

China's U curve-shaped trend of income differential change was not obvious in the past 20 years, and in the total differentials, we only saw that a turning point was realized in 1996, in which the income differential degree realized a steady trend. In some fractional analyses, the income differential change truly presented a mild U curve trend in certain categories. Moreover, in the analysis of China's differential formation mechanisms and reasons presented in the next chapter, we will also see that this U curve situation is obvious in the income distribution of employed people in the private sector.

It should be noted that as compared with developed countries, China's development of income differential polarization was quite quick. According to the analysis of Alderson *et al.* (2005), from 1969 to 1999, Britain's polarization MRP index was less than 0.2, and the United States' MRP was less than 0.15. In China, from 1988 to 2007, over only 20 years, the MRP index reached 0.2035 without considering household population, and reached 0.2450 when considering the household population. Prior to this comparison, we did not know how high China's polarization degree of income differentials was. Without adjustment in China's income differential, it is unthinkable to what the degree of polarization will reach in the future.

Chapter 7

Children of the Reform and Opening Up

Tian Feng

Since the reform and opening up, the Chinese society has experienced huge changes; people's modes of conduct, lifestyle, and values have undergone profound modifications. These changes have had left an indelible influence on the Chinese youth's growth and development; this new generation and their modes of conduct and value orientation will surely affect the future of China.

I. Concepts of "Youth", "Post-1980s", and "Generation"

The group classified as the "children of the reform and opening up" has included two phenomena of interrelation. "Generation" is an important method to divide up groups in sociology, much like the class, stratum, race, and gender. In common usage, "generation" has three different kinds of meanings: first is the intergenerational relations produced by age difference, such as youths and elders; second is the intergenerational relations produced by blood relationships, such as grandparent or offspring generations; third is "generations" defined by common ideas and behavioral characteristics, such as "the fifth generation of directors" and "post-1980s generations".

Regarding the definition of youth, a unified standard has not been formed domestically and abroad. But whatever the standard, age is the key factor to define youth. The United Nations Educational, Scientific, and Cultural Organization (UNESCO) once stipulated that "youth" pertains to people aged between 14 and 34 years (in 1982). The World Health Organization (WHO) stipulated that youth refers to people aged between 14 and 44 years (in 1992); the United Nations Fund for Population Activities (UNFPA) stipulated that youth refers to people aged between 14 and 24 years old (in 1998). In China, the National Bureau of Statistics stipulated that youth refers to people aged 15 to 34 years (census). According to related stipulations of the Communist Youth League, youth refers to people aged 14 to 28 years ("Regulation of Chinese Communist Youth League"). The All-China Youth Federation stipulated that youth refers to people aged 18 to 40 years ("Regulation of All-China Youth Federation"). The related organizations of Hong Kong, Macao, and Taiwan stipulated that youth refers to people aged 10 to 24 years (Hong Kong Commission on Youth, Macao Statistics and Census Service, Taiwan National Youth Commission).

The phrase "post-1980s" expresses not only the "youth generation" born in the 1980s, but also a "special generation" that has distinct characteristics of the time. The "post-1980s" youth truly refracts huge social changes, and it is not only a concept of "age grouping", but also a concept of "social grouping".

With rapidly increasing social change, the intergenerational age range is also reducing; therefore, the media have started using phrases such as "post-1970s" ("70后" — 70 *hou*, people born in the 1970s), "post-1980s" ("80后" — 80 *hou*, people born in the 1980s), and "post-1990s" ("90后" — 90 *hou*, people born in the 1990s), which actually refer to the generations after reform and opening up, or the one-child generations. The studies on the influence of big social events, modes of conduct, and values of the youth generation are an important subject of sociology. American sociologist GH Elder once conducted groundbreaking research in this aspect of generations; he explained the influence of the global Great Depression from 1929 to 1933 on children's development using survey data accumulated by the California Auckland Adolescent Growth Study; his basic data was the record of long-time follow-up observations from the 1930s to the

1960s on 167 Americans born in Auckland, California between 1920 and 1921. His outstanding research findings were collected in a book titled *Children of the Great Depression*, his research indicated that major social events such as depression, war, and extreme social disturbances can reshape an individual's life course; some people thereby suffered numerous setbacks in life, while some had unexpected opportunities (Elder, 2002). Thereafter, the relationship between social change and an individual's life course have become an important research subject of sociology. Zhou Xueguang (周雪光) and Hou Liren (侯立仁) introduced this subject into the body of research on contemporary China in a paper "Children of the Cultural Revolution — Contemporary China's national and life course"; they studied the influence of the movement "in the countryside" during Cultural Revolution. They investigated the youth generation using the national representative resident samples of 20 cities and discovered that this influence was continuous and had different influences on children of different social strata (Zhou Xueguang and Hou Liren, 2003).

Different from the "children of the Great Depression" and "children of the Cultural Revolution", the "children of the reform and opening up" did not grow up in such adverse circumstances but rather in a favorable period. Their youth and growth environment were completely different than that of their elders. They lived in a gradually open environment and were widely influenced by Western culture and lifestyle. They experienced a deepening of the market economy, which placed them in an atmosphere of competition and profit seeking. Their living standards also increased significantly, hardly suffering the adversities and frustrations of prior generations. Most of the population in this generation is also a product of the single-child policy. This environment created some distinct characteristics, which led them to become a unique generation in the modern history of China.

Many academic circles have already started to pay attention to this generation of people who grew up in the era of reform and opening up; the domestic media frequently calls them "post-1970s", "post-1980s", and "post-1990s". From the attention on the "Little Emperor" phenomena ("小皇帝" *xiao huang di* — refers to Chinese only-child generation born in the 1980s) to calling them the "Hedonist generation" ("享乐的一代" *xiang le de yi dai*) which "drinks Coca-Cola and eats hamburgers", and to the discussion on the *"Xiaozi* generation" ("小资一代" *Xiao zi yi dai* — similar to Yuppie), and the "Indignant youth generation" ("愤青一代" *fen qing yi dai*); all these trends reflect Chinese people's understanding and portrayal of the behavioral characteristics of the generation born after reform and opening up.

For the "children of the reform and opening up", at first the media and society as a whole pointed out faults and criticized them; for example, they said this was "the most irresponsible generation", "the most selfish generation", "the most rebellious generation", and "the most coddled generation". The "post-1980s" generation was thought to be a generation that was not concerned about politics and did not care about society because they lived in a more open world, had not experienced struggle and pain, had blind faith in foreign goods, enjoyed Japanese cartoons and South Korean soap operas, made a fuss about imaginary illnesses, and sought melancholy and sadness in their lives of affluence. After the Wenchuan earthquake in 2008, people's viewpoint on this generation changed; in the face of this national calamity, the "post-1980s" generation manifested their high national spirit, social compassion, and sense of responsibility and established the mission of their time with their selfless dedication and spirit of cooperation.

This chapter's core subject is the main group characteristics of the "children of reform and opening up". What characteristics do their ideology and value orientation have? Particularly, what influence will their sense of justice and democratic consciousness have on China's future?

II. Data Sources and Research Methods

This chapter's data is from CSS made by the Institute of Sociology and the Chinese Academy of Social Sciences from May to September, 2008. This survey covered 135 counties (city, district) in 28 provinces (municipalities, autonomous regions), 260 townships (town, street), and 520 villagers' and residents' committees. The surveyors visited over 7,100 households, obtained 7,139 effective questionnaires, and the survey error was smaller than 2%, which met the scientific requirements of statistical inference. The questionnaire contents included not only basic information, such as age, sex, income, and occupation but also related additional information, such as the behaviors and social attitudes.

This section defines the "children of the reform and opening up" as the group born after the 1970s and differentiated them into two groups: "post-1970s" and "post-1980s". As compared with the section of other age groups, such classifications and definitions also considered this generation's differences in social behavior, lifestyles, and values from other age groups. After screening, the sample of 2,286 people was in accordance with conditions in the cruising data.

Because the "children of the reform and opening up" grew up in a special social reformation period, and their modes of conduct were definitely influenced by the ensuing social changes, they can have largely different modes of conduct than previous age groups; therefore, the features and behavioral characteristics of the "children of the reform and opening up" are reflected in their social attitudes, particularly their attention and anxieties of current social contradictions. This chapter attempts to look for the "children of the reform and opening up", who have a unique sense of justice and democratic consciousness.

Democratic consciousness and sense of justice were measured through indicators composed by two groups of questions. The question of measuring the democratic consciousness was "what degree can you agree following views?" The questions included 12 options: the public place is a place that individuals do not need to be responsible for; the government needs to relocate residential housing for reconstruction; the common people should obey the government, and the subordinate should obey their leaders; democratic governments should take responsibility for the decisions of the people; the affairs of the state should be administered by the government, and the common people do not need to consider such things; letting a small number of people become rich first is not good for society; some people will be wealthy, while others are poor, which is fair; few cadres wholeheartedly consider the common people; many bosses get rich due to government officials' help; in our society, workers' and farmers' children have the same opportunities as other people's children to become rich and gain higher status; farmers should focus on farming and not enter the cities for work; and more taxes should be levied from the rich to help the poor. The answers included five options: disagree, less agree, agree, fully agree, and do not know.

The questions on measuring the sense of justice are: what is the degree of justice in the following aspects currently? The questions includes

13 options: the income differential, job opportunities, the college entrance examination system, selecting party and government cadres, public medical services, compulsory education, political rights of citizens, the judicial system and law enforcement, the development differential between different areas, the treatment differential between different industries, the treatment differential between urban and rural residents, social security, and social justice as a whole. The answers included five options: very unfair, less fair, fairer, very fair, and do not know.

III. "Post-1970s" and "Post-1980s" Youth's Principal Characters

As "children of the reform and opening up", "post-1970s", and "post-1980s" youth have many different characteristics from former groups; these characteristics were formed in specific historical conditions and were also the result of changes in economy, politics, culture, and other external conditions in the youth's socialization process. From the attention on "Little Emperor" phenomenon in the 1980s to calling them the "Hedonist generation", and to the following discussion on "Xiaozi", "Indignant youth", and the "NEET group" ("啃老族" *keng lao zu*, namely the "boomerang" children). This indicated that, as compared with the former crowd, the present-day youth has their own characteristics of behavior. In the present-day youth's characteristics of education, work, and income, there are close relations (Wang Xiaotao (王晓焘) and Hu Feng (胡丰), 2008). Under the influence of new media trends, these younger generations pursue novel lifestyles based around consumption and entrust modern phenomena with greater social meaning (Zheng Hong'e (郑红娥), 2006).

A. *Educational qualifications and the income on the rise*

The "post-1970s" and "post-1980s" youth's average levels of education were, respectively, 9.5 and 11.2 years; there has been a constant and obvious growth trend since the 1960s (see Figure 7.1). This has much to do with the popularization of higher education, whether it is the increase of college enrollment or the increase in graduate school enrollment. Considering some

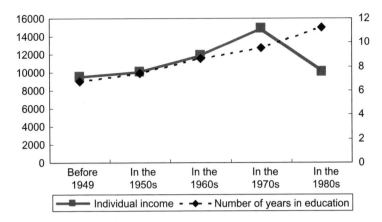

Figure 7.1. Average Income and Years of Education by Age Group.

"post-1980s" generation is still in school, it may be foreseen that "post-1980s" average level of education will be even higher as they complete more schooling.

According to the human capital theory, the level of education has very important influence on income. From the data analysis, we can also see that, although the "post-1980s" had the highest average level of education, "post-1970s" actually had the highest average income; this is because many of the "post-1980s" generation have not yet entered the job market. Even if some have entered employment, their seniority is not yet high. As the "post-1980s" generation's seniority gets enhanced, it is hopeful that their average income level will surpass the "post-1970s" generation.

B. *Proportion of employment in public ownership units has obviously dropped*

Under the planned economy system, the proportion of employment in public ownership units was high, and the urban employment in state-owned and collective enterprises was the main employment structure. After the reform and opening up, the non-public economy grew largely, and has become an indispensable economic sector in the national economy; simultaneously, the proportion of employment in public ownership units has obviously dropped. Our analysis discovered that people born in

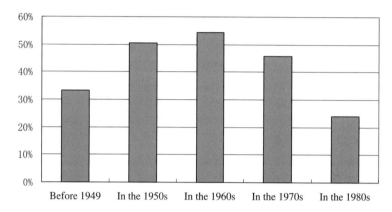

Figure 7.2.   Proportion of Employment in the Public Ownership Unit by Age Group.

the 1960s had the highest proportion of employment in public ownership units, and the "post-1970s" generation's proportion was lower than that of people born in the 1950s and 1960s in terms of public ownership units. The "post-1980s" generation had the lowest proportion in the public ownership unit; only about 24% of the "post-1980s" generation was working in public ownership units (see Figure 7.2). This indicated that the employment has also presented more privatized characteristics along with economic and social development, and government jobs were no longer the youth's only choice.

C. *Young people tend toward new fashions and trends*

Lifestyle can be an important factor in defining the difference between groups and social strata (Li Chunling (李春玲), 2004). Generally, it is thought that the "post-1970s" and "post-1980s" youth's lifestyles are obviously different from other age groups because they grew up after China's reform and opening up. This chapter's analysis has also verified the particularity of the "post-1970s" and "post-1980s" generations in terms of life style. As compared with former research, the analysis discovered that this particularity was not "broken", but presented trends and rules of change from "pre-1970s" to "post-1970s" and then to "post-1980s" generations.

In terms of the three aspects of "clothes", "food", and "behavior", the "post-1980s" generation is not only the group most likely to purchase clothes in brand name stores, emporiums, and online but also the group most likely to choose dining out in fast-food restaurants, and most opt for

Table 7.1.   Various Age Groups' Life Style.

Lifestyle	Before 1949	During 1950s	During 1960s	During 1970s	During 1980s
Where do you often buy your clothing?					
Brand specialty store	2	3.05	5.04	9.61	20.43
Online shopping	0.35	0.24	0.15	0.71	2.16
Emporium	10.63	11.46	13.80	19.36	25.88
Where do you often eat?					
Fast-food restaurant	2.79	3.78	6.39	11.46	17.37
General restaurant	4.18	6.40	8.18	12.24	13.51
Few dining out	71.17	63.96	55.79	42.35	34.28
What is your way to go out?					
On foot	56.62	48.96	42.18	36.87	40.75
Drive/by private car	1.57	1.89	3.63	5.62	3.75

Note: Units: %.

cars or motorbikes instead of walking. As a result, the "post-1980s" youth do not have much money in savings (see Table 7.1).

In terms of the proportion using media, the older the interviewees were, the more likely they used traditional media. People born in the 1950s and before 1949 watched TV nearly every day, listened to the radio, and read the newspaper, at proportions obviously higher than other age groups. The new youth use more fashionable media. The proportion of the "post-1970s" generations which reported using the internet and SMS messages every day was obviously higher than people born before the 1970s, and the proportion of the "post-1980s" youth who read periodicals and magazines, browsed the internet, and received and sent SMS messages every

Table 7.2. Proportion of Various Age Groups Using Media.

Proportion of almost doing following activities every day	Before 1949	In 1950s	In 1960s	In 1970s	In 1980s
Watching TV	81.18	83.54	77.53	78.43	69.69
Listening to the radio	9.42	6.40	3.92	4.70	4.77
Reading the newspaper	23.63	20.67	17.09	22.22	18.62
Reading periodicals and magazines	2.79	3.35	3.49	4.63	8.29
Browsing the internet	2.26	4.21	6.83	15.10	27.24
Receiving and sending SMS message	1.92	5	10.65	22.01	44.38

Note: Units: %.

day was highest. Therefore, in terms of changing trends, the "post-1980s" lifestyle has not broken the trend of younger generations seeking new age media (see Table 7.2).

D. *Young people favor expressing their own opinions*

The social attitude of groups is an important topic in sociological research. Some people were not willing to answer questions on social attitudes, or chose the "Do not know" option to avoid sensitive issues in the survey. There was the special column of social attitude in the questionnaires of the CSS 2008 in which, except for the senses of democracy and justice, it also involved the degree of satisfaction and sense of security, totaling 42 questions. For each of these questions, some interviewees chose "Do not know". Chen Chengwen and Peng Guosheng ((陈成文) and (彭国胜), 2006) thought that the reason for these answers can be traced back to the current structure of "social systems" and cultural contradictions. The analysis discovered that the number of times choosing "Do not know" in all options had strong correlation with age; interviewees 40 years old and above chose "Do not know" much more regularly. Moreover the phenomenon presented an unceasing upward trend along with age as a whole (see Figure 7.3).

If interviewees are divided into three groups "pre-1970s", "post-1970s", and "post-1980s", it is found that the average number of times people chose "Do not know" was respectively, 2.6, 1.94, and 1.67 times, the analysis of variance also indicated these three groups had obvious

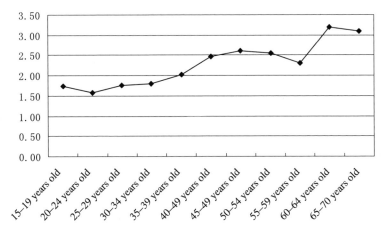

Figure 7.3. Mean Value of Answering "Do Not Know" by Age Group.

differences. Great disparity between the "pre-1970s" generation and the other two groups was created possibly because of the absence of information, but the difference between "post-1970s" and "post-1980s" generations was possibly due to the difference in the desire to express opinions.

IV. "Post-1970s" and "Post-1980s" Youth's Sense of Justice and Democratic Consciousness

After the reform and opening up, as a result of Western values and marketization permeating Chinese culture, young people's values have undergone huge changes from prior generations. Li Yunyun ((李云赟), 1990) reported that the youth's democratic consciousness development from reform and opening up to 1989 could be divided into four phases: awakening, thinking, practice, and confusion. Ke Ruiqing ((柯瑞清), 1996) reported that at that time youth's consciousness change presented a trend of marketability, secularization, and utilitarianism. Weng Dingjun ((翁定军), 1999) reported that the sense of justice was a result of new social norms and social criterion internalized on individuals. Zhang Guang and Liu Weiwei's ((张光) and (刘伟伟), 2008) studies discovered that, as compared with procedural unfairness, in the situation of procedural fairness, college students had a higher degree of satisfaction with the result. In the overwhelming majority of circumstances, the procedure and the result jointly influenced college students' sense of justice. Democratic consciousness and the sense of justice both belong to the category of social consciousness. "Democratic consciousness" is the general name of a democratic viewpoint and is often manifested in the reconsideration of former politics and requirements of the realpolitik,[1] along with transformation or improvement of socio-economic structures. The sense of justice pays attention to reasonable dispositions between people and things, namely how the individual stands in society and mode of distribution of public wealth and resources. At the same time, the sense of justice can also measure people's sense of just treatment and benefit sharing between individuals and groups, as well as understanding the opportunities of fairness and fairness in processes and results.

According to the analysis of the cruising data, "post-1970s" and "post-1980s" youth did not display an obvious difference in their sense of justice and democratic consciousness; in some studies and groupings, the "children of the reform and opening up", the "post-1970s", and the "post-1980s" youth were regarded as the same group.

A. *"Post-1970s and post-1980s" youth's sense of justice and democratic consciousness are more intense*

In the analysis of social justice, "post-1970s" and "post-1980s" youth had the most intense sense of China's income differential; another concern was about labor treatment differentials among different industries. Except for income differential and treatment differential among different industries, the development differential among different areas in China and the rights and treatment differentials between urban and rural residents were also considered unfair. The national institutional arrangements can often help bring about a higher degree of satisfaction; this includes compulsory education, the college entrance examination system, and public medical service. The questions concerning the national judicial administration were easier to be avoided, and the questions on law enforcement and selecting party and government officials had the highest proportion of "Do not know" choices.

---

[1] Jia Ping'an (贾平安) and Hao Shuliang (郝树亮) (1993), *The Glossary of United Front Science*. Beijing: Social Sciences Academic Press.

Table 7.3. Difference Between Sense of Justice Among "Post-1970s and -1980s" Youth and "Ante-1970s" Group.

Whether fair is following aspects or not?	Group	Very unfair	Less fair	Fairer	Very fair	Do not know
Income differential	Post-1970s and -1980s	26.16	42.61	25.11	3.46	2.67
	Ante-1970s	24.95	43.79	24.52	3.09	3.65
Job opportunities	Post-1970s and -1980s	14.70	39.94	34.43	6.34	4.59
	Ante-1970s	12.01	39.30	35.34	5.15	8.20
College entrance examination system	Post-1970s and -1980s	3.32	9.19	48.25	26.25	12.99
	Ante-1970s	2.12	7.17	49.82	24.99	15.89
Selecting party and government cadres	Post-1970s and -1980s	11.68	29.13	37.49	8.62	13.08
	Ante-1970s	11.29	28.09	38.31	7.93	14.37
Public medical service	Post-1970s and -1980s	4.64	23.23	54.59	10.98	6.56
	Ante-1970s	4.86	21.90	56.44	10.01	6.78
Compulsory education	Post-1970s and -1980s	1.84	8.84	55.38	30.80	3.15
	Ante-1970s	1.59	7.85	56.81	27.80	5.96
People's political right actually enjoyed	Post-1970s and -1980s	6.21	21.43	48.95	14.74	8.66
	Ante-1970s	3.98	18.75	52.54	14.01	10.72
Judicature and law enforcement	Post-1970s and -1980s	7.96	28.48	42.91	8.62	12.03
	Ante-1970s	6.80	24.97	44.61	8.35	15.27
Development differential among different areas	Post-1970s and -1980s	14.57	40.46	30.58	5.25	9.14
	Ante-1970s	11.42	37.54	33.24	5.17	12.63
Treatment differential among different industries	Post-1970s and -1980s	17.32	40.29	28.83	5.12	8.44
	Ante-1970s	15.35	37.98	30.37	5.11	11.19

(*Continued*)

Table 7.3. *(Continued)*

Whether fair is following aspects or not?	Group	Very unfair	Less fair	Fairer	Very fair	Do not know
Right and treatment differentials between urban and rural residents	Post-1970s and -1980s	13.87	39.15	35.17	4.90	6.91
	Ante-1970s	11.72	37.91	35.71	5.34	9.31
Treatment of social security such as endowment insurance etc.	Post-1970s and -1980s	11.55	29.05	42.13	7.48	9.80
	Ante-1970s	10.82	29.98	43.68	6.45	9.07

Note: Units: %.

Comparing "post-1970s and -1980s" youth with "pre-1970s" interviewees, these two groups were basically consistent in terms of their sense of injustice, but the "post-1970s and -1980s" youth had significantly higher proportions in choosing "very unfair" than "pre-1970s" interviewees (see Table 7.3).

Both groups' consciousness of their democratic rights was similar to their sense of justice; "post-1970s and -1980s" youth was basically consistent with the "pre-1970s" group, but had a higher degree of these feelings. On the question, "the public place is a place that individuals do not need to be responsible for", 41.9% youths chose "disagree", which was 13% higher than the "pre-1970s" interviewees; on the question "the affairs of the state should be administered by the government, and the common people do not need to excessively consider such things", 18% of youths chose "disagree", which was 9% higher than "pre-1970s" interviewees. These figures indicated that the youth have a stronger sense of individual responsibility. On two questions, "the government should relocate residential housing for reconstruction, and the common people should move out" and "farmers should farm well, and not enter the city for work", 12.5% and 47.9% of "post-1970s and -1980s" youths, respectively, chose "disagree", which were higher by 4% and 11.5% than "pre-1970s" interviewees, respectively. This indicated that youths' consciousness and feelings toward rights were also more intense (see Table 7.4).

Table 7.4. Difference Between Democratic Consciousness of "Post-1970s and -1980s" Youth and "Ante-1970s" Group.

Whether democracy is following aspects or not?	Group	Disagree	Less agree	Agree	Fully agree	Do not know
The public place is such place that individuals do not need to be responsible for	Post-1970s and -1980s	41.91	39.06	13.12	3.15	2.76
	Ante-1970s	28.54	42.53	19.25	3.73	5.96
If the government needs to relocate residential housing for reconstruction, the common people should move out	Post-1970s and -1980s	12.47	36	37.71	10.15	3.67
	Ante-1970s	9.62	31.32	41.62	11.91	5.52
The common people should obey the government, and the subordinates should obey the superior	Post-1970s and -1980s	9.23	31.36	43.70	13.78	1.92
	Ante-1970s	5.54	21.64	49.54	19.88	3.40
A democracy is a government that takes the responsibility of a decision for the people	Post-1970s and -1980s	6.65	19.77	47.03	22.66	3.89
	Ante-1970s	4.45	15.68	50.09	24.48	5.30
The affairs of the state should be administered by the government, and the common people do not need to consider them	Post-1970s and -1980s	17.98	38.23	29.48	11.59	2.71
	Ante-1970s	8.96	31.61	40.16	15.76	3.50
Letting a small number of people become rich first is not good for society	Post-1970s and -1980s	12.77	44.14	30.05	8.92	4.11
	Ante-1970s	7.69	36.02	38.45	10.49	7.36

(Continued)

Table 7.4. (*Continued*)

Whether democracy is following aspects or not?	Group	Disagree	Less agree	Agree	Fully agree	Do not know
Now some people make lots of money, and some make little, but this is fair	Post-1970s and -1980s	9.41	26.73	45.14	16.49	2.23
	Ante-1970s	8.26	25.61	46.49	15.15	4.49
Now few cadres wholeheartedly consider the common people	Post-1970s and -1980s	3.67	16.05	41.86	35.35	3.06
	Ante-1970s	2.88	16.13	45.02	31.61	4.35
Many bosses get rich because of government officials' help	Post-1970s and -1980s	3.98	26.07	40.29	22.13	7.52
	Ante-1970s	2.84	19.58	45.35	22.75	9.48
Worker and farmer's children have the same opportunities as other people's children to become rich and have status	Post-1970s and -1980s	8.18	24.98	43.83	20.12	2.89
	Ante-1970s	7.17	24.62	45.48	17.43	5.30
Farmers should farm well, and should not enter the city for work	Post-1970s and -1980s	47.86	34.21	12.86	4.07	1.01
	Ante-1970s	36.33	37.58	17.16	6.22	2.70
More taxes should be levied from the rich to help the poor	Post-1970s and -1980s	3.24	18.68	41.56	33.20	3.32
	Ante-1970s	2.18	12.63	45.56	35.24	4.39

Note: Units: %.

B. *Factor analysis of "post-1970s and -1980s" youth's sense of justice and democratic consciousness*

To facilitate the following analysis, the data need to be simplified; therefore, we analyzed 24 questions on the sense of justice and democratic consciousness using the method of factor analysis and handled the option of "Don't know" as an absent value and deleted some information. Finally, 1,532 cases were included in the factor analysis, in which 926 were "post-1970s" interviews, which accounted for approximately 60% of the cases, as well as 606 "post-1980s" interviews, which accounted for approximately 40% of the cases; both were basically consistent with the overall trends.

According to the results of the factor analysis, this chapter retained only two factors which had characteristic values greater than 1. Among them, the youth's sense of justice and the youth's democratic consciousness represented factors 1 and 2, respectively. The cumulative contribution rate of these two factors was 95.57%, which means that these two factors can explain 95.57% of the differences in all variables (see Figures 7.4).

We analyzed the two factors' scores and discovered that the distribution of the two factors approached normal distribution. Therefore, the factor score may be analyzed as the dependent variable. In fact, through verification, factor 1 was completely in accordance with the hypothesis of normal distribution, but factor 2 was skewed to a certain extent, only after deleting some outlying values could it meet the requirements of normal distribution.

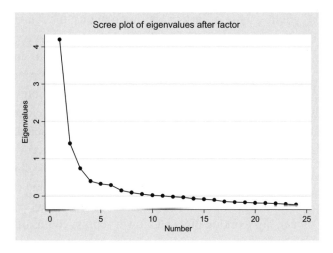

Figure 7.4. Factor Analysis Results on "Post-1970s and -1980s" Youth's Sense of Justice and Democratic Consciousness.

This chapter transformed the factor score into a standard scale of 0–100 points, in which a higher score of factor 1 represented the interviewees' stronger sense of justice, whereas the lower score of factor 2 represents the interviewee's stronger democratic consciousness and emphasized personal liability. Because the distribution of factor 2 presented skewed values, when processing, we set the mean value at 50, which allowed some interviewees to score above 100.

C. *Influence of different factors on "post-1970s and -1980s" youth's sense of justice and democratic consciousness*

Generally speaking, although scores had certain differences after being separated into different types, "post-1970s" and "post-1980s" youth's sense of justice and democratic consciousness had similar scores; only a few classifications had different influences. In the following text, we will make comparative analysis of "post-1970s" and "post-1980s" youth's sense of justice and democratic consciousness aiming at the different factors of influence.

The types of household registration and the unit system are often regarded as the institutional factors of social structure. In terms of the division of institutional factors, the difference between "post-1970s" and "post-1980s" youth's sense of justice was not obvious; the sense of justice and democratic consciousness of youth in rural households scored slightly lower than those from non-rural households; the sense of justice and democratic consciousness of youth in the public ownership unit scored slightly higher than non-public ownership units. The scores between "post-1970s" and "post-1980s" youth's democratic consciousness had obvious differences; "post-1970s" youth's democratic consciousness was distinctly higher than "post-1980s" youth, which indicated that "post-1980s" youth paid more attention to individual rights. The institutional factors also similarly caused bigger differences in democratic consciousness; the democratic consciousness of youths in non-rural households and non-public ownership working units had lower scores; youths of non-rural household registration and non-public ownership working units were less constrained by the government and the system and, therefore, emphasized individual function to a greater extent.

The two factors of area and gender did not cause obvious differences between the "post-1970s" and "post-1980s" youths, but "post-1980s" youth displayed stronger uniformity. The sense of justice of "post-1970s" youth in the eastern region had the highest score, but the difference between areas was not very big. "Post-1980s" youth's sense of justice did not present much difference among regions of China. The score of democratic consciousness of "post-1970s" youth increased progressively in the eastern, central, and western regions, which was opposite the direction of the sense of justice. The gender difference was mainly manifested in the sense of justice; among "post-1970s" and "post-1980s" youth, men scored higher than women.

Income is an influencing factor that most possibly shapes perception of social injustice; generally, the lower the income, the more the group feels there is social injustice. In fact, the influence of income on "post-1970s" youth is that the higher the income, the lower the sense of justice scored. Low-income youth favor to think that the society was just. We compared "post-1970s" with "post-1980s" youth's scores and discovered that the difference in the sense of justice mainly came from middle-income groups; particularly "post-1970s" youth's scores were obviously lower than those of the "post-1980s" youth, thus indicating that "post-1970s" youth with a higher income were actually more concerned with social injustice than other groups. In terms of influence of income on democratic consciousness, there was no clear trend; whereas higher income groups tended to approve more of government power, lower income groups tended to support individual rights.

The level of education had an effect on both income and social consciousness. In terms of the sense of justice, the difference caused by education was not distinct, but the sense of justice for those with an education, such as graduate student or those who had higher education, was significantly higher than other groups. In terms of democratic consciousness, the graduate student group was distinct; other than the graduate student group, "post-1970s" and "post-1980s" youths presented the situation where, the higher the educational qualifications, the lower they scored on democratic consciousness, which indicated that an increase in level of education can make youth more aware of the importance of individual rights (see Table 7.5).

Table 7.5. "Post-1970s" and "Post-1980s" Youth's Sense of Justice and Democratic Consciousness.

Classification	Sense of justice		Democratic consciousness		Classification	Sense of justice		Democratic consciousness	
	Post-1970s	Post-1980s	Post-1970s	Post-1980s		Post-1970s	Post-1980s	Post-1970s	Post-1980s
Public ownership	49.92	50.78	49.03	46.64	Rural household registration	49.67	49.88	50.10	45.22
East	51.03	50.50	44.58	42.34	Without regular education	46.74	47.33	63	62.70
Central	49.99	49.57	47.99	45.78	Elementary school	48.29	45.21	52.49	50.60
West	48.22	50.44	49.19	43.74	Junior high school	50.56	50.46	46.81	46.18
Man	51.20	51.43	46.32	43.75	Senior high school	49.95	51.36	43.87	41.56
Woman	48.93	48.92	47.67	43.76	Vocational senior middle school, technical secondary school	50.30	50.74	42.93	40.62
20% of highest income	45.90	48.46	48.36	43.64	Junior college	50.09	49.55	40.31	40.67
20% of higher income	47.63	50.91	52.40	46.81	Bachelor	52.34	51.15	39.70	40.50
20% of middle income	50.78	48.28	45.92	45.28	Master	56.93	55.68	44.34	43.32
20% of lower income	51.41	52.07	46.15	42.29	Members of Chinese Communist Party and Communist Youth League	49.63	50.08	47.44	43.80
20% of lowest income	52.26	53.04	42.53	40.86	Without the political status	53.60	54.35	42.21	41.83

Note: Unit: %.

The influence of the interviewee's political status was also meaningful; as compared with members of the Chinese Communist Party and Communist Youth League, youth without political status favored to think that the society was just. Youth without political status favored emphasis on individual rights, which was distinctly different from the score of democratic consciousness of youth without political status. Youth with political status were obviously more constrained with organizational requirements of obedience toward the government and nation.

D. *Cluster analysis to youth's sense of justice and democratic consciousness*

The aforementioned analysis discovered that the difference between "post-1970s" and "post-1980s" youth's sense of justice and democratic consciousness was not very obvious; thus, "post-1970s" and "post-1980s" youth may be regarded as a group having similar social attitudes. Many factors influence the youth's sense of justice and democratic consciousness; therefore, it is difficult to conduct classified research regarding the youth's sense of justice and democratic consciousness, and other variables must be introduced to carry on auxiliary classifications. This chapter has chosen level of education and income as the subsidiary variables of classification, which are also helpful to differentiate the type of youth with the aid of the interviewee's other information.

After introducing the variables of levels of education and income, the units and the interval between variables were inconsistent; therefore, it was necessary to make respective variable values not to inundate other variables through some form of standard linear transformation. This paper used the method of range standardization, and each variable was divided by its own range. Though there was a need to classify more than 1,500 cases into "types", we actually had no standards to determine how the classification should be done. These divisions were ungrounded as there was the probability that each type can contain similarities, which means that certain "types" of youth cluster around different scales after classification; therefore, the method of weighted averages is more significant and meaningful.

The preliminary results of the cluster analysis revealed that the majority of clusters occurred when diversity scores were lower than 0.8; moreover,

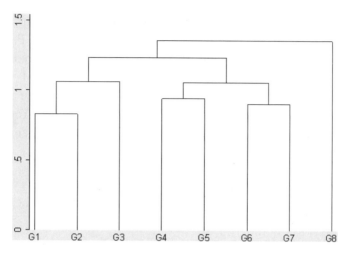

Figure 7.5. Result of Cluster Analysis on Youth's Sense of Justice and Democratic Consciousness.

many would be unable to truly realize the needs of the type. Therefore, we adjusted the conditions given for analysis, and only considered the clusters in which the diversity was higher than 0.8 (see Figure 7.5).

According to the cluster results, this paper traced the cluster process and discovered that G8 (Group 8) was a special type of group; it only clustered toward other groups when the diversity was greater than 1.2. The analysis discovered that the number of G8 cases was only 3; the average level of education was 13.3 years and the average annual income surpassed RMB 320,000; the average scores for the sense of justice and democratic consciousness were 64.7 points and 36.8 points, respectively; this group featured high educational qualifications and income and tended to think that society was fairer; most also emphasized individual rights. Further analysis discovered that these three cases were employers; two were private businessman and one was a small businessman. Therefore, G8 may be thought to be representative of the emerging young private businessman.

G1 to G3 on the left side of Figure 7.5 mainly represented the low-income youth group, in which G2 was also a special type of youth. G2's sense of justice score was lowest, at only 34.3 points; of all nine groups, this group considered society as least just. Further analysis discovered that average level of education of G2's 11 cases was 13.3 years and had an average annual income of RMB 4,000, among which seven G2 cases had no job. They were representatives of the youth group that received higher education, but were still unemployed. In the current society, as post-college unemployment is common, this group is the most likely to claim society is unfair. G3 is a similarly low-income group, and this was the least educated group. Although most of them were employed but income was low; the average income was also only slightly more than RMB 4,000. Their scores for sense of justice actually reached as high as 65 points, which was obviously higher than G2. Through the comparison of G2 and G3, it may be thought that higher levels of education will lead to greater sense of injustice.

G5 had the highest scores in their sense of justice; their average level of education was 15.7 years, and their average income exceeded RMB 150,000. This group is representative of youth group that obtained high income because of high educational qualifications. G7's average level of education and income were not high, at respectively 9.8 years and RMB 12,700, but their sense of democratic consciousness had the highest score of any group; the analysis discovered that as many as 44% of them worked in the public sector, which was largely higher than 36% overall average. This group was representative of youth working in the public sector; they had stable income and a higher level of dependency on the government; therefore, they had relatively less of a demand for individual rights (see Table 7.6).

Table 7.6. Result of Cluster Analysis on Youth's Sense of Justice and Democratic Consciousness.

Group	Score of fairness factor	Score of democracy factor	Average educated number of years	Average income (RMB)
G1	Middle	Middle	7.6	8,020
G2	Low	High	13.3	4,417
G3	Middle	High	6.1	4,808
G4	Middle	Low	13.7	18,183
G5	High	High	15.8	155,008
G6	Middle	Middle	9	12,138
G7	High	High	9.8	12,701
G8	Middle	Low	13.3	323,333

V. Main Conclusions and Policy Suggestions

The "children of the reform and opening up" are in the process of huge social changes and rapid social reform; they have formed a generation that has obvious intergenerational difference from previous generations. In comparing the "pre-1970s", "post-1970s", and "post-1980s" youths, there are obvious characteristic differences; their income and educational qualifications are higher, their lifestyles tend to be more modern and fashionable, and they favor expressing their own opinions. At the same time, their social attitude is obviously different than other groups, mainly in their sense of justice and democratic consciousness; they tend to think that society is unfair and emphasize individual rights and responsibility. Although the majority of "post-1970s" youth were not born after reform and opening up, their growth process has actually inevitably been marked by reform and opening up; their modes of conduct and values are quite similar to the "post-1980s" generation in some ways.

In the comparative analysis of "post-1970s" and "post-1980s" youth's sense of justice and democratic consciousness, some external factors, such as system, income, and political status have big influence. For instance, youth without the status of membership of the Chinese Communist Party of the Communist Youth League favored emphasis on individual rights and had distinctly different scores of democratic consciousness from youth with political status. Youth of non-rural households and of non-public ownership units had low scores regarding democratic consciousness, which illustrates that the government has different influences on different groups, and youth of non-rural households and non-public work groups were less restricted by the government. Therefore, they emphasized individual function and responsibility. In most situations, the difference between "post-1970s" and "post-1980s" youths is relatively small. For instance, the two groups presented a trend in which level of education was determinant of their sense of democratic consciousness and individual rights.

The difference of social attitudes between "post-1970s" and "post-1980s" youth was not obvious; the variables of income and education were introduced to attempt a more thorough analysis. The analysis discovered that there were some special groups in the youth; G8 was representative of young private sector businessmen, who had both high educational qualifications and high income and tended to think that society was fairer; they also emphasized individual rights to a greater extent than other groups. Through the comparison of G2 and G3, we also discovered that G2 had a higher level of education but lower income levels; they felt society was unfair. While G3's income was also low, they did not receive as much education and did not expect to obtain high returns from education. They tended to think that society was relatively fair. Groups that worked in the public sector did not have high income and had a certain level of dependency on the country; this group had the least demands in terms of individual rights.

As a whole, although the "post-1970s" youths had certain differences from "post-1980s" youths in terms of lifestyle, the change in social structure has also created special youth groups; "post-1970s" and "post-1980s" youths have high uniformity in social attitudes. Therefore, in view of current youth's sense of justice and democratic consciousness, this chapter makes following four suggestions:

(1) Avoid labeling "post-1980s" youths and help them to integrate into the mainstream society

    This research did not discover any obvious differences in social attitudes between "post-1970s" and "post-1980s" youth; this proves that it is wrong for some organizations and media to label the "post-1980s" group. Although the "post-1980s" group is possibly different than mainstream society in terms of lifestyle, we see that their environment is unprecedented. With the lapse of time and growth, their lifestyle will change gradually; prejudice toward them will likewise gradually decline. Therefore, we should avoid labeling "post-1980s" youths and help them to integrate into mainstream society.

(2) Positively push the employment of graduates to eliminate their intense sense of injustice

    The imbalance between educational structure and employment structure after university education has caused problems for graduates looking for employment. Education can give a better sense of society; however, they are unable to obtain the corresponding income return from higher education which will hugely increase the youth's sense of injustice and frustration. Measures should be taken to strengthen the guidance and alleviate the employment pressures of graduates to avoid the psychological toils of unemployment. Graduates who cannot get a job after graduation should receive help in finding employment in order to attenuate their views on the social injustice. Graduates should be encouraged to start working in such basic work units to gain an appreciation for the values of life and education.

(3) Emphasize young pioneers' responsibility consciousness and guide them to serve society

In recent years, establishing businesses for youths became important work of the Party and Youth League organizations and government organizations; the research discovered that some youths who successfully established a business had an intense consciousness of individual rights and responsibilities. Therefore, according to young pioneers' strong responsibility consciousness, youths should be encouraged to establish businesses in order to contribute to social and economic development. Young pioneers should be encouraged and led to serve society and to play leading roles; they should be regarded as a kind of latent social resource to be cultivated and discovered, and a batch of young entrepreneurs who have responsibility and concerns should be built up according to corresponding support policies.

(4) Cultivate youth's correct understanding of democratic rights

Emphasizing citizen's democratic rights is an important condition to build a harmonious society. The research discovered that young people who have a high level of education and work in the private sector have a more intense consciousness of individual rights and responsibilities; therefore, the youth's education of democratic ideals should be further pursued. Youths should be led to correctly exercise individual democratic rights to enhance the youth's understanding of democracy so that they can maintain independence and exercise their democratic rights; youths should be encouraged to undertake responsibility independently, and the principle that the collective interests are higher than personal interest should be emphasized.

Conclusion: Research Findings and Further Problems

Li Peilin

I. Main Research Findings

A. *Consumption is mainly influenced by the income, public services, social security, and income distribution*

The research analysis indicated that China's consumption is mainly because of the influences of four aspects: first is the influence of the resident income; as compared with government financial revenue and the incomes of enterprise and unit, the proportion of resident income continues to be reduced relative to the entire national income. Therefore, resident consumption is depressed. Second is the influence of insufficient public services; the survey discovered that, in terms of household consumption, consumer expenditures in education and medical services displayed strong rigidity; this not only has a squeezing effect on other consumer expenditures that have suppressed normal family consumer expenditures but has also increased families' savings, adversely affecting domestic demand. Third is the influence of insufficient social security; inability to retire and cover medical and unemployment expenses are objects of resident's savings plans. Fourth is the influence of income distribution structure; the survey discovered that household consumption decreased successively along with income increase; the oversized income differential resulted in a structure that did not lend to domestic consumption increases. The findings indicated that high-income house-holds' consumption rates were basically fixed, while rural and low-income families' marginal propensity to consume was high, although their actual purchasing power was limited. The survey also discovered that although rural families' consumption of durable goods, such as home appliances, was higher than their urban counterparts, rural consumption was relatively depressed because of the limitations of income and social security.

B. *Attention must be paid to non-regular employment, the second generation of migrant laborers, vocational education, and the statistical monitoring*

The survey discovered that in the current labor market, the non-regular employment market is huge; employment cost is low, employment elasticity is big, and the non-regular employed group accounts for about 50% of all non-agricultural employed people. In the past, China paid great attention to support full-time regular employment, as against non-regular flexible employment. Insufficient supervision has caused an excessively high threshold of non-regular employment and a high frequency of labor dispute cases. Job enlargement teamed with better supervision should vigorously promote non-regular employment, which will create good conditions for businesses and independent operators.

The survey also discovered that, since 2000, the second generation of migrant laborers who have entered the labor market were different from the first generation. They not only pay attention to income increases but also aim to improve their own and their children's social status to a greater extent. Migrant laborers are more often bringing their children with them, migrant laborers' "returning to their native village, but not for farming" has become an important characteristic; the pattern of unidirectional movement — settlement in cities promulgated by the traditional urban and rural population movement theory has evolved into a pattern of bidirectional flowing out — backflow — settlement under China's new national conditions. The union of migrant laborers' movement and settlement in cities will have important influences on China's urbanization and non-agricultural development.

The research indicated that in the labor market, the difference in incomes was mainly influenced by human capital factors, such as educational level, technical ability, and work experience. Worker's social security was mainly influenced by institutional factors, such as household registration and work units. Therefore, raising primary workers' income level should start through improving worker quality. In recent years, China's general secondary education and higher education have rapidly developed; but comparatively speaking, vocational education development actually has been reduced, the quality of student sources has dropped, and the staffing has decreased. In recent years, China's vocational education has been restored, but there is much room for improvement. Adjusting higher education structure and speeding up the development of vocational education and vocational training will be necessary to adapt to the changing labor market and to improve primary workers' income level.

The unemployment rate is an important basis to reflect economic development and the readjustment of interest rates, tax rates, and wages. At present, China's urban registered unemployment rate has fallen behind and is insufficient to reflect the changes of the labor market accurately. The special system of statistics, monitoring, and announcement for urban investigated unemployment rates should be set up according to the international unemployment rate statistics specifications so that the unemployment rate targets may become the main basis of macroscopic policy-making.

C. *Migrant laborer group, the popularization of medical security, and the future old age risks should be taken seriously in the social security program*

China's present social security system is mainly designed, managed, and operated according to two kinds of urban and rural socioeconomic formations, and the urban and rural dualistic structure is obvious, but the migrant laborer group has become the lost group of social security. The survey indicated that migrant laborer's coverage rate was universally low; therefore, how to design a social security system that can link urban and rural areas and that conforms to the characteristics of migrant laborer's movement is a key to establish an effective social security system covering urban and rural areas.

The analysis discovered that in all kinds of social security, as compared with endowment insurance and unemployment insurance, medical insurance had more obvious effects in improving worker's social security treatment in the non-regular employment market. This is possibly because the majority of non-regular employed people's employment is flexible. Solving the problem of the medical coverage is an urgent matter. In establishing and consummating the social security system covering urban and rural areas, consummating and enhancing medical security should be regarded as an ultimate goal to be vigorously pursued.

At present, China's population is aging; the total quantity of seniors living by themselves without a spouse is rapidly increasing along with the decline in birth rates. The survey indicated that one-third of one-person and two-person households were composed of people 60 years and older; moreover, the lower the family income, the higher was the dependency ratio of the family's elders. The reshaping of family structure has seriously challenged the traditional way of retirement, and the funds for retirement security will face swift growth of pressure in the future. While establishing a medical security system covering urban and rural areas, China must not only carry on the tradition of familial old age support but also pay attention to the security of old people living alone. At present, the age structure of the endowment insurance program is older than the labor force's age structure; therefore, the age structure of the insured should be adjusted through the expansion of endowment insurance coverage to avoid latent risks of a depressed endowment insurance fund.

D. *Social construction needs to restructure the social support network*

In the process of social reform, the social support network has had profound changes; because of the transformation from "work unit staff" to "social being" that occurred in market reform, the structure of the original planned economy condition has become attenuated. The social support system also needs time to mature. The modernization reforms have changed China from an acquaintance-based society into a public-based society. The personal social support network based on blood relationships and geographical location formed in the acquaintance society has become less influential. As a result, China must now need to build a social support network to adapt to this huge social change.

The survey discovered that, at present, China's social support network depends more on the personal relationship network and less on family. The development of non-relative personal relationships in the social support network has been very quick; the "community" has substituted for the "work unit" in organized social support to become the organized support strength that aids most residents. The support provided by the community (villagers' committee and residents' committee) occupied two-fifth of total organized support; transformation from "the work unit undertaking social responsibility" to "the community serving the society" has caused the community to become the main provider of organized support resources in society. Some supports attenuated by "the system of work units" are being shared by the community, local government, party, and mass organizations. In terms of the support strength toward members, the function of community support was still lower than work unit support. The survey also showed that a family's per capita income assumed an inverse correlation with the quantity of organized support; the lower the household income, the higher was the organized support strength obtained. At present, China's social support mainly gives priority to economic support; families that obtain economic support are increasing along with the reduction of income.

In establishing a social support network to adapt to social reform, community construction should be strengthened vigorously, social work should be positively pushed, specialized organizations of social service should be cultivated, the work unit's support role should be continued, and the social security of the public service system of widespread coverage should be constructed.

E. *Labor's comparative superiority will more likely be manifested in labor's quality in the future*

With China entering a new stage of industrialization, industrial structure is upgrading unceasingly; the contribution of technical progress to economic growth has become more distinct, and the requirement for labor's technical abilities has also greatly increased. Therefore, migrant laborers must adapt to this new requirement in the future. With changes of labor supply, the era of low-cost Chinese labor will gradually end and China's future economic growth must realize the transformation from "Made in China" to "Chinese branding". From this analysis, we may see that migrant laborers' education level and technical abilities were still somewhat low relative to urban staff; moreover, this has also had decisive influence on migrant laborers' income level. At present, the overwhelming majority of migrant laborers only have the educational level of junior middle school; therefore, migrant laborers' skills should be enhanced through the formulation and implementation of large-scale vocational education and vocational training. This is a strategic choice considering the overall situation of economic and social development, and social labor productivity should be hugely enhanced through large-scale labor quality enhancement. This will satisfy the requirement for China's industrial structure to improve along with its standings in the global economic pattern.

F. *Historical logic decides migrant laborers' positive social attitude*

According to the analysis of the cruising data, comparatively speaking, migrant laborers have a more positive and enterprising social attitude; this is mainly decided by the historical logic of the constant rise of migrant laborers' income. The pressure of the international financial crisis and economic recessions have had a negative influence on migrant laborers' social attitudes toward the social security system, their sense of social justice, and their degree of satisfaction with the government. Their pressures in life are mainly from threats to their employment, not from their income level. Therefore, migrant laborers' employment security must be taken seriously and solved. The analysis discovered that, in all kinds of social security, medical insurance for urban employees and the new rural cooperative medical system have had the most obvious effects on migrant laborers' living conditions and social attitude. Therefore, in the process of pushing the construction of the social security system covering urban and rural areas, while positively consummating various social security systems, consummating migrant laborers' medical security should be regarded as a priority to enhance migrant laborers' social security level.

In the past three decades, migrant laborers' working and living conditions as well as their social attitudes were important factors in affecting the overall situation of Chinese economic and social development. In China's development over the next three decades, their working conditions, living conditions, and social attitude will be important factors in affecting the overall situation of reform, development, and stability.

G. *Family old age support will be still China's main body of retirement support*

With China's profound changes in social structure, the family structure also presents the tendency of nuclear structure and simplification. The decline in mortality rate, the lengthening of per capita life expectancy, the improvement of housing conditions, the quickening of social movement, as well as the changing intergenerational relations all have lent to a massive increase in older generations living by themselves, unassisted. China's traditional intergenerational old age support pattern has been unprecedentedly challenged. According to our survey, only 9.74% of urban old people explicitly expressed that their children had helped them substantially in the past year, with this proportion being only slightly higher at 14.22% in rural areas. At the same time, 49.7% of urban seniors were covered by basic endowment insurance for urban residents, and 12.3% were covered by their former employer's supplementary endowment insurance. Rural retirees still depended almost totally on family; this structure faced multiple problems in which children's economic support was limited for parents and grandparents. In this case, many scholars thought that China's retirement pattern development should change from family-based support to social, community-based support.

According to our analysis of the cruising data, we discovered that family scale's reduction, which caused a drop in a family's ability to provide old age support, and the population bonus, which brought by the fast drop in fertility rate instead, reduced the dependency coefficient of family populations. The urban family's population dependency was in cycle of rising; average population dependency of each employed person rose from 1.73 people in the mid-1990s to 1.93 people in 2006. The rural family's population dependency was in a cycle of decline; average population dependency of each laborer dropped from 1.64 people in the early-1990s to 1.43 people in 2006. This indicated that the family scale's reduction does not necessarily reduce Chinese families' old age support abilities. The main pattern of old age support in the future will still be that of family support and the duty to support parents should be advocated in the entire society, the standards of filial piety that are advantageous for old age support in the traditional culture should be emphasized, and harmonious intergenerational old age support should be guaranteed by the necessary economic, social, cultural, and educational means.

II. Issues Discussed Further

A. *Issues regarding mass consumption*

This research report has shown that China has entered a new stage of development, and the first characteristic is the arrival of mass consumption. The stage of mass consumption that was thought to be distant in the 1990s and early 2000s, has, in fact, arrived. China's per capita GDP increased from more than US$300 to more than US$800 from 1980 to 2000; since then per capita GDP surpassed US$1,000 in 2003, then it surpassed US$2,000 in 2006, and amounted to more than US$3,300 in 2008, which had realized the goal set by the government 12 years ahead of their timeline set in 2000. This kind of rapid development had something to do with three factors, namely fast economic growth, the reduction of net population increase, and the RMB revaluation. The Engel's coefficient of resident consumption was dropping continually, and the proportion of food consumption in total urban household consumer expenditures actually dropped to about 30% because the housing expenditures were underestimated. Various countries' experiences indicated that the mass consumption stage has arrived if the Engel's coefficient drops to about 30%; at this stage, a large amount of consumables, including housing and cars, start to become ubiquitous and new consumption in education, medical services, traveling, and communication become points of growth for consumption. A stage mass consumption has arrived, and research is insufficient at this point; the understanding of this phenome-non is still not understood in China.

In some scholars' opinion, it is no doubt good to expand domestic con-sumption, but it needs time to develop; it is difficult to stimulate economic growth through consumption in the short term. Therefore, investment in sustainable domestic consumption should be taken seriously. Moreover, generally it is thought that a high savings ratio and high investment rate are China's national condition. Therefore, the transformation of develop-ment should mainly be concerned with how to change the investment structure and enhance investment results. This hypothesis actually means that development mainly depends on investment in the previous 30 years and continuous development will depend on continuous investment.

We first look at the hypothesis "it is very difficult to stimulate economic growth by the consumption in a short term". This hypothesis seems ini-tially to make sense, but it is questionable after thorough consideration. First, this hypothesis is based on past development experiences; under the condition of economic growth rate in the past, the economy receives stimu-lus through finance and investment expansion, never through consumption expansion. It was not that China did not have such a desire; it simply never realized such a result. When stimulating the economy through high invest-ments after a crisis, there is a great risk of redundant projects, capacity surplus, surplus in inventories, and a decline of investments, all causing inflation. Therefore, after this international financial crisis, there is no say-ing whether these unsolved problems will repeat themselves.

China must seek new possibilities and a kind of new future. China's economic and social development has entered a new growth stage; this stage's characteristics are different from the past. Previously, there have been three big factors promoting economic growth: investment, exports, and consumption; from now on, China should aim for long-term steady economic growth by increasing domestic consumption.

B. *Issues regarding the gradual end of low-cost labor*

The employment trend change has something to do with the problems of low-cost labor. Labor's supply-demand relationship is experiencing fluc-tuating changes. Due to the aging population structure, there is a declining supply of labor; an estimated 6 million new laborers will enter the market annually from 2006 to 2010, which will decline to 3 million every year from 2011 to 2015. An inflection point will come around 2016. Employment is not only affected by events, such as the international financial crisis, but also sees problems in years of fast economic growth.

This is caused by labor market division; with the upgrading industrial structure, the primary blue-collar labor market requires more and more knowledge and technical abilities. Some migrant laborers become excluded from the non-agricultural labor market because they are unable to adapt to these new requirements. Simultaneously, white-collar labor market growth is slow and cannot catch up with the swift growth of graduate populations. Therefore, the labor market will present a situation in which a labor shortage and unemployment could coexist in the future.

To solve this problem, China must rapidly develop rural education, vocational education, and vocational training to satisfy the requirement for industrial upgrading through improvement of labor quality. Non-regular employment channels of the white-collar labor market should be gradually expanded. According to our research, encouraging flexible employment is an important measure to deal with unemployment. At present, China's non-regular employed people occupies approximately 50% of total non-agricultural employed population, but the overwhelming majority of them are concentrated in the blue-collar labor market. Regarding the self-employed and non-regular employed people, the low threshold principle should be taken, procedures for business autonomy should be simplified, good conditions of businesses should be created for independent operators, and simultaneously the supervision of labor rights protection should be strengthened.

At present, the household registration system and the division of urban and rural employment markets in large and medium-sized cities have set up barriers keeping migrant laborers from settling in areas; owing to this, migrant laborers are unable to settle down and obtain employment in large or medium-sized cities and about 25% of migrant laborers ultimately have return to their native village to farm. China's household registration system reform will be helpful for non-agricultural employed rural residents to leave the farm permanently and will promote the synchronized development of rural non-agriculture employment and urbanization.

C. *Issues on the expansion of China's income differential*

Income differentials in China are an issue of serious concern. Presently, there is no feasible research to clearly explain the rules of income differential expansion in the past three decades, as well as projections for future trend. The theory that was frequently cited to explain the issue of China's income distribution is American Economist Kuznets' hypothesis for forecasting the changing trend of income differentials in the future. The Kuznets hypothesis was based on research of income differentials in developed countries in the 50 years before the Second World War (Kuznets 1955). According to the hypothesis of Kuznets theory, the changing trend of income distribution should start to present an inverse U curve, which first expands and then reduces. In actuality, although China has taken a series of special operational policy measures to reverse income differential expansion trends, the possibility that the income differential curve presents an inflection point has yet to be seen. Moreover, according to our analytical study, the rural income inequality was always higher than that of urban areas, the agricultural sector's income inequality was always higher than the non-agriculture sector, and the structural effects of income inequality were higher than the centralized effects in the majority of years, which are contrary to the parameters defined by the Kuznets hypothesis.

In the process of China's income differential expansion, in the mid-1990s, the phenomenon that "the price of brainwork is lower than or equal to the price of manual labor in same working hours" appeared in the initial period of income differential expansion ended. In recent years, with the slow growth of market wages because of severe competition, the situation that the average level of market wages was higher than the financial wage level was also changed. However, the analysis results on the source of income showed that, the closer the relations between the source of income and the marketization, the bigger the influence to the income inequality. The contribution of the income inequality of employed people in the private sector to the overall inequality was largely greater than the contribution of public sector workers in income inequality. The complications faced in reversing the income differential's expansion trend are more complex; through state power, China not only needed to rectify the inequalities brought by marketization using finance, tax revenue, social security, and social welfare, but also needed to prevent the inequality caused by the power-money union using the market's competitive mechanisms. It is troubling that the additive effects of market inequality and authority inequality appear; therefore, a kind of social mechanism must be built to simultaneously restrict market inequality and authority inequality as well as the union of both.

D. *Issues on social stratification and mobility*

Social mobility is the people's change of social position; migrant laborers represent social mobility from agricultural to urban skilled and semi-skilled work. Since reform and opening up, China's social mobility has sped up. The argument's focus is whether increasing social mobility is still continuing, and whether there are still opportunities through this unceasing reorganization. Scholars are exploring whether the process of social differentiation has basically ended, and if the social stratum structure has become concretely defined.

Through the analysis of the cruising data, we seemed to have obtained contradictory results. Objectively, Chinese society is still in the process of social mobility acceleration; there are many spaces and opportunities for social mobility, particularly with the popularization of higher education, the influx of government employees, business management personnel, and intellectuals. However, the agricultural workforce is aging. According to our survey, in China's vocational strata, the proportion of farmers was 42% but is undergoing dramatic decline. Through the analysis of the cruising data, we discovered factors that affect people's economic and social status. With the rise of educational capital influence, parents' social and economic status has also become another influencing factor, as well as the household registration system. Education has had an important influence on children in obtaining social and economic status, and this influencing factor had played a vital role in children obtaining the education resources and employment.

This result tells us that China's industrialization and urbanization are also in an accelerating period; the structural change elasticity is still very high. Profound changes of social vocation will unceasingly create space and opportunities for new social position promotion and enable the overwhelming majority of people to have the ability to increase their social standing and reshape China's social environment and stability. The large-scale social stratum reorganization process seems to have ended; some situations of social stratum duplication have begun to appear. It is helpful to overcome structural instability, but it can form the structural tension and suppress structural vigor, thus, having negative influence on efficiency and fairness in social movements.

E. *Issues regarding the "children of the reform and opening up"*

Famous sociologist GH Elder's *Children of the Great Depression* has become a classic to analyze the influence of big events' effects on individuals' life courses. However, "children of the reform and opening up", namely "post-1970s" and "post-1980s" young people are completely different from "children of the Great Depression" or "children of the Cultural Revolution". Three conditions caused the "children of the reform and opening up" to become a special generation: first, the birth control policy caused them to be an "only-child" generation and to receive unusual family care and social attention; second, the favorable circumstances and relatively comfortable living conditions that developed after reform and opening up have caused them to lack individual experiences and collective memories of frustrations in the past; third, China's marketization, informatization, and globalization environment after reform and opening up have reshaped their culture and knowledge structure. This generation was often criticized as "the most irresponsible generation", "the most selfish generation", "the most rebellious generation", and "the most coddled generation" by the domestic media, while the overseas media thought that they were a generation of "radical nationalism". However, the Wenchuan earthquake in 2008 changed people's views, the "post-1980s" generation manifested high national spirit, social compassion, and a sense of responsibility in the face of national calamity and accepted the mission of the times with their selfless dedication and cooperative spirit.

Our research indicated that as compared with their parents' generation, the "children of the reform and opening up" have on average a higher income level and educational qualifications, work in the private sector, tend toward a modern lifestyle, and favor expressing their own opinions. At the same time, their social attitudes, mainly in their sense of fairness and democratic consciousness are obviously different from other crowds.

In brief, the "children of the reform and opening up" will become China's elite strength in development over the next 30 years to support China's sustainable development; their knowledge quality, collective consciousness, and mental outlook will decide China's future development trends.

F. *Issues on China's development power*

Since reform and opening up began 30 years ago, China has introduced the socialist market mechanism through economic restructuring. The market mechanism has provided equality of competitive opportunities, thus, mobilizing various social strata for development investment, and ultimately bringing about a greater level of vigor in the total population. The benefit pattern has had profound change, income and property differentials are expanding unceasingly, and people are dissatisfied with distribution injustices; in order to solve this problem, the mechanism for fair benefit distribution should be further developed through social restructuring to impel China's development. Other concerns tied to this are tying together democratic rights and an effective socialist political system that can deal with all kinds of challenges and complex aspects to create a more reliable political structural reform to provide new development power. Economic opportunity equality, social benefit fairness, and political rights are three sides of the same issue; the current reform must begin with the economic domain and move into the social domain and political realm ultimately providing new, stronger potential for China's future development.

Bibliography

Alderson, Arthur S., Beckfield, Jason and Nielsen, François (2005). "Exactly how has income inequality changed? Patterns of distributional change in core societies". *International Journal of Comparative Sociology* 46 (4), pp. 405–23.

Antonucci, Toni C. and Kees C.P.M. Knipscheer (1990). "Social Network Research: Review and Perspectives." pp. 161–173 in *Social Network Research: Substantive Issues and Methodological Questions*, K. C. P. M. Knipscheer and T. C. Antonucci (eds.). Amsterdam: Swets & Zeitlinger.

Bai Xuemei (白雪梅) (2004). "Education and income inequality: An empirical study in China", *Management World* (6), pp. 53–58.

Bian Yanjie (边燕杰) (eds.) (2002). *Market Transformation and Social Stratification — An American Sociologist's Analysis on China*. Shanghai: The Joint Publishing Company.

Bian Yanjie (边燕杰) and Zhang Wenhong (张文宏) (2001). "Economic institutions, social networks, and career mobility", *Social Sciences in China* (2) pp. 77–89.

Bian Yanjie (1997). "Bringing strong ties back." *American Sociological Review* (62) pp. 366–85.

Burt, Ronald S (1984). "Network items and the general social survey." *Social Networks* (6) pp. 293–339.

Cassel, J (1976). "The contribution of the social environment to host resistance." *American Journal of Epidemiology* (104) pp. 107–23.

Chen Chengwen (陈成文) and Peng Guosheng (彭国胜) (2006). "Aphasia in an unbalanced world — sociological analysis on loss of peasant workers' right to speak", *Tian Fu New Idea* (5), pp. 93–97.

Chen Guangjin (陈光金) (1996). *Review and Prospect of Rural Modernization in China*. Changsha: Hunan Publishing House.

Chen Guangjin (2005). "From elite circulation to elite copying — evolution of the main mechanisms of the formation of private employers in China", *Study & Exploration* (1), pp. 44–51.

Chen Nabo (陈那波) (2006). "Overseas literature reviews of the debates on China's market transformation for 15 years", *Social Studies* (5), pp. 188–212.

Chen Qiuhua (陈秋华) *et al.* (2002). *System Conversion — Structural Changes and Employment.* Beijing: China Financial & Economic Publishing House.

Chen Xiaoyu (陈晓宇), Chen Liang (陈良) and Xia Chen (夏晨) (2003). "Changes of urban educational earning rate in the mid 1990s and enlightenment", *Peking University Education Review* (2), pp. 65–71.

Chen Xiwen (陈锡文) (2009). "20 million unemployed peasant-workers return to their native villages, the government actively responds", http://news.xinhua-net.com/politics/2009-02/02/content_10750425.htm.

Chen Zhiwu (陈志武) (2006). Can state ownership and government regulation really promote balanced development? — political economy of revenue opportunity (January 2). *The Economic Observer.*

Chen Zongsheng (陈宗胜) (1991). Income distribution in economic development. Shanghai: SDX Joint Publishing Company.

Chen Zongsheng (陈宗胜) (1991). *Income Distribution in the Economic Development.* Shanghai: Joint Publishing House.

Chen Zongsheng (2000). "Thorough studies on income distribution differences in China — a review of 'studies on income distribution differences in China'", *Economic Research Journal* (7), pp. 68–76.

Chen Zongsheng and Zhou Yunbo (周云波) (2001). "Influence of illegal non-normal income on income differences and its economic interpretation", *Economic Research Journal* (4), pp. 14–23.

Cobb, S (1976). "Social support as a moderator of life stress." *Psychosomatic Medicine* (38) pp. 300–314.

Dan Guangnai (单光鼐) (ed.) (1994). *Report on Chinese Youth Development.* Shenyang: Liaoning People's Publishing House.

Ding Renzhong (丁任重), Chen Zhizhou (陈志舟) and Gu Wenjun (顾文军) (2003). "'Inverted-U hypothesis' and income gap in the China's transitional period", *The Economist* (6).

Du Yang (都阳) and Gao Wenshu (高文书) (2005). "How far China is from unitary social security system", *China Labor Economics* (2), pp. 45–59.

Du Yuhong (杜育红) and Sun Zhijun (孙志军) (2003). "Education, income and experiences of labor market in China's underdeveloped areas", *Management World* (9), pp. 68–75.

Eastwood, R., and Lipton, M (2004). "Rural and Urban Income Inequality and Poverty: Does Convergence between Sectors Offset Divergence within Them?"

in G. A. Cornia, *Inequality, Growth and Poverty in an Era of Liberalization and Globalization*. Oxford: Oxford University Press for UNU-WIDER.

Elder, GH (2002). *Children of the Great Depression*, Tian He (田禾) and Ma Chunhua (马春华) (translators). Nanjing: Yilin Press.

Feng Xiaotian (风笑天) (1994). "One-child family: A new life style", *Social Science Journal* (5), pp. 28–32.

Fischer, Claude S (1982). *To Dwell among Friends*. Berkeley: University of California Press.

Fu Ling (傅玲) and Liu Guibin (刘桂斌) (2008). "Approaches to resolve income polarization", *Statistics and Decision* (13), pp. 135–136.

Gu Jianping (顾建平) (2003). *Studies on Unemployment and Employment Changes in China*. Beijing: China Agriculture Press.

Guan Xiaoming (管晓明) (2006). "Deduction of inverted-U hypothesis and tests in China", *Journal of Shanxi University of Finance and Economics* (5), pp. 24–27.

Guo Fei (郭飞) (2005). "New thoughts on the principle of production factors participating in distribution according to contribution", *Marxist Studies* (2), pp. 26–62.

Guo Xibao (郭熙保) (2002). "The Kuznets hypothesis from the perspective of development economics — causes of income inequality expansion in China", *Management World* (3), pp. 66–73.

Han Liufu (韩留富) (2009). "Unceasing expansion of income gap in the Yangtze delta", *Yangtze Delta* (3).

He Keming (赫克明) and Wang Ming (汪明) (2009). "One-child policy and education reform — report on China's one-child studies", *XinHuaWenZhai* (10).

He Wei (何伟) (2006). "Injustice of resource allocation decides unfairness of income distribution — another discussion on equity cannot be related with distribution closely", *China Business and Market* (7), pp. 10–13.

He Ya (何娅) (2007). "Gini coefficient: Deconstruction of urban and rural historical policies", *China National Conditions and Strength* (4), 23–27.

He Zhaiping (贺寨平) (2004). *Social Network and Living Conditions: Investigation on Social Support Network of the Rural Elderly*. Beijing: Chinese Social Science Press.

Hong Xingjian (洪兴建) and Li Jinchang (李金昌) (2007). "Reviews of polarization measurements and income polarization", *Economic Studies* (11), 139–153.

Hong Yongtai (洪永泰) (1996). *Studies of the Sampling Within Household.* Taipei: Wu-Nan Book Publishing Company.

House, J. S., D. Umberson, and K. R. Landis. (1988). "Structures and processes of social support." *Annual Review of Sociology* (14) pp. 293–318.

Hu Daiguang (胡代光) (2004). "Analysis of new liberalism and its consequences of implementation", *Contemporary Economic Studies* (2), pp. 17–21.

Jiang Guocheng (江国成) (2009). "National development and reform commission: Establishment of a socialist market economic system in China", xinhuanet.com (on October 5).

Jiangsu Provincial Bureau of statistics (2007). "Analysis of the distribution of wages for staff and workers in cities and towns in Jiangsu province", *China Statistical Information Network* (on October 17, 2007).

Jin Xizai (金喜在) (1996). *Studies on Contemporary Resident Income Distribution in China.* Changchun: Northeast Normal University Press.

Ke Ruiqing (柯瑞清) (1996). "Changes of youth's consciousness and its orientation", *Journal of Party College of Fujian Province Committee of CCP* (6), pp. 62–66.

Knight, J., and Song, L. (1999). *The Urban-Rural Divide: Economic Disparities and Interactions in China.* New York: Oxford University Press.

Kuznets, Simon (1955). "Economic growth and income inequality". *American Economic Review* 45 (1), pp. 1–28.

Kuznets, S (1989). *Modern Economic Growth (1966),* Dai Rui (戴睿) and Yi Cheng (易诚) (translators). Beijing: Beijing Economic College Press.

Lai Desheng (赖德胜) (1999). Education, labor market and income distribution. In *A Study on Resident Income Distribution in China,* Zhao Renwei (赵人伟) *et al.* (eds.) Beijing: China Financial & Economic Publishing House.

Lai Desheng (2001). *Education and Income Distribution.* Beijing: Beijing Normal University Press.

Lee, Rance P. L., Ruan Danqing, and Gina Lai. (2005). "Social structure and support networks in Beijing and Hong Kong." *Social Networks* (27) pp. 249–274.

Levin, HM (1995). Equal educational opportunity and social inequality in Western Europe. In *Technology, Benefits, Financing and Reform — Major Issues in Education Policy and Management,* HM Levin. Beijing: The People's Daily Press.

Li Chunling (李春玲) (2003a). "How education level affects income — current economic earning rate of education", *Social Studies* (3), pp. 64–76.

Li Chunling (2003b). "Social and political changes and unequal educational opportunity — effects of family background and institutional factors on education (1940–2001)", *Social Sciences in China* (3), pp. 86–98.

Li Chunling (李春林) (2004). "Social class identity", Jiangsu Social Sciences, (6) pp. 108–112.

Li Chunling (2004a). *Fragmentation: An Empirical Analysis on the Social Stratification of the Contemporary China*. Beijing: The Social Sciences Academic Press.

Li Chunling (2004b). "Social stratification in China and new trend of life style", *Scientific Socialism* (2), pp. 12–15.

Li Peilin (2001). "Support network for social lives — from *Danwei* to community", *Jiangsu Social Sciences* (1) pp. 53–55.

Li Peilin (2006). "From traditional safety to modern risk", *China Economic & Trade Herald* (1–2) pp. 143–144.

Li Peilin and Zhang Yi (张翼) (2000). *The Analysis of Social Costs of State-Enterprises in Transitional China*. Beijing: Social Sciences Academic Press.

Liang Qin (梁勤), Mi Jianwei (米建伟) and Zhang Qi (章奇) (2006). Income gap between rural residents in China and its policy implications — evidence from farmers in six provinces, candidate paper in the First Elites Competition for Economic and Management Papers, Samsung Economic Research Institute China.

Li Shi (李实) (2000). "Further interpretations of issues in the studies of income distribution — reply to the comments of professor Chen Zongsheng", *Economic Studies* (7), pp. 72–76.

Li Shi and Ding Sai (丁赛) (2003). "Long-term changes in private returns to education in urban China", *Social Sciences in China* (6), pp. 58–72.

Li Shi and Li Wenbin (李文彬) (1994). Estimates of the private rate of return to education investment in China. In *Studies on Household Income Distribution in China*, Zhao Renwei (赵人伟) and Keith Griffin (eds.). Beijing: The China Social Science Press.

Li Shi and Luo Chuliang (罗楚亮) (2007a). "Re-estimating the income gap between urban and rural households in China", *Journal of Peking University (Philosophy and Social Sciences)* (2), pp. 111–120.

Li Shi and Luo Chuliang (2007b). Income differentials and social equity, Annual Report on Reform (2007) by China Institute for Reform and Development (CIRD) China.

Li Shi, Zhao Renwei and Zhang Ping (张平) (1998). "Absolute and relative standards of 'Polarization'", *Management World* (1), pp. 40.

Li Shi and Zuo Tenghong (佐腾宏) (2004). *The Costs of Economic Restructuring — Empirical Analysis on Urban Unemployment, Poverty and Income Differentials in China*. Beijing: China Financial & Economic Publishing House.

Li Peilin (李培林) (1996). "The social network and social status of migrant workers", *Social Studies* (4), pp. 42–52.

Li Peilin (ed.) (2003). *Migrant Workers: The Economic and Social Analysis on China's Migrant Workers in Cities*. Beijing: Social Sciences Academic Press.

Li Peilin and Chen Guangjin (2008). Making vigorous efforts to turn the situation: China's social development takes new challenges — general report on analysis and forecast on China's Social Development (2008–2009). In *Analysis and Forecast on China's Social Development (2009)*. Social Sciences Academic Press.

Li Peilin, Chen Guangjin, Zhang Yi and Li Wei (2008). *Report on China's Social Harmony and Stability*. Social Sciences Academic Press.

Li Peilin *et al.* (2005). *Social Conflicts and Class Consciousness*. Beijing: Social Sciences Academic Press.

Li Peilin and Li Wei (李炜) (2007). "Economic status and social attitudes of migrant workers in the transformation of China", *Social Studies* (3).

Li Peilin and Li Wei (2008). Survey Report on the People's Livelihood in China (2008). In *Analysis and Forecast on China's Social Development (2009)*. Social Sciences Academic Press.

Li Peilin and Zhang Yi (张翼) *et al.* (2000). *Employment and Institutional Changes: Job-seeking Process of Two Special Groups*. Zhejiang People's Publishing House.

Li Qiang (李强) (1993). *Social Stratification and Mobility in Contemporary China*. Beijing: China Economy Press.

Li Qiang (2003). "The influence of thrust and pull factors on China's rural-urban floating population", *Social Sciences in China* (1).

Li Xinhua (李新华) (1989). "Youth and adults: Future dual social structure", *Contemporary Youth Research* (3).

Li Yunyun (李云赟) (1990). "'78 To '89 the evolution of democratic consciousness of university students ", *China Youth Study*, (5) pp. 22–24.

Li Yunyun (李云赟) (1990). "Evolution of college students' awareness of democracy in 1978–1989", *China Youth Study* (5).

Lin Yifu (林毅夫), Cai Fang (蔡昉) and Li Zhou (李周) (1998). "Analysis on regional disparities in the economic transformation of China", *Economic Studies* (6).

Lin Youping (林幼平) and Zhang Shu (张澍) (2001). "Overview of income distribution in China since the 1990s", *Economic Review* (4).

Liu Guoguang (刘国光) (2005). Increased attention to social equity (April 16). *The Economic Information Daily*, pp. 5.

Liu Jinming (刘精明) (1999). "Effects of the 'Cultural Revolution' on entering high school and enrollment patterns", *Social Studies* (6).

Liu Jinming (2005). *Country, Social Strata and Education: Sociology of Education*. Beijing: Renmin University Press.

Liu Jinming (2006a). "Expansion of higher education in China and inequality in entrance opportunities: 1978–2003", *Society* (3).

Liu Jinming (2006b). "Structural changes in the labor market and human capital gains", *Social Studies* (6).

Liu Xin (刘欣) (2005). "Multiple power foundation of social stratification in current China — an interpretation of power derivative theory", *Social Sciences in China* (4).

Lu Feng (路风) (1989). "Danwei: a particular form of social organization", *Social Sciences in China* (1) pp. 71–88.

Lu Jiarui (卢嘉瑞) (2002). "Income gap and polarization", *Journal of Hebei University of Economics and Trade* (3).

Lu Xueyi (陆学艺) (ed.) (2001). *Social Strata Studies in Contemporary China*. Social Sciences Academic Press.

Lu Xueyi (2004). *Social Mobility in Contemporary China*. Beijing: Social Sciences Academic Press.

Marsden, Peter V (1987). "Core discussion networks of Americans." *American Sociological Review* (52) pp. 122–31.

Ma Guangqi (马广奇) (2000). "Analysis and measurement of China's economic marketization process", *Qiu-Shi* (10).

Ma Xiaohe (马晓河) (2003). "Analysis on income inequality", *Hong-Qi* (16).

Marx and Engels (1995). *Karl Marx and Frederick Engels*. People's Publishing House.

Mead, GH (1988). *The Generation Gap*, Zeng Hu (曾胡) (translator). Guangming Daily Press.

Nielsen, François and Alderson, Arthur S.(1997). "The Kuznets curve and the great U-turn: Income inequality in U.S. counties, 1970 to 1990". *American Sociological Review* 62(1), pp. 12–33.

Ning Deye (宁德业) and Pang Yejun (庞业君) (2007). "Thoughts on whether to have polarization in current China", *Productivity Research* (6).

Polany, K (2007). *The Great Transformation: The Political and Economic Origins of Our Times*, Feng Gang (冯钢) and Liu Yang (刘阳) (translators). Zhejiang People's Publishing House.

Ruan Danqing (阮丹青), Lu Zhou (周路), Peter Blau, Andrew Walder (1990). "A priliminary investigation of social networks of urban residents in Tianjin", *Social Sciences in China* (2) pp. 157–176.

Ruan, Danching, Linton Freeman, Xinyuan Dai, Yunkang Pan, and Wenhong Zhang(1997). "On the changing structure of social networks in urban China." *Social Networks* (19) pp. 75–89.

Shi Meixia (石美遐) (2007). *Studies on Labor Relations of Irregular Employment.* China Labor and Social Security Publishing House.

Shultz, TW (1990). *On Human Capital Investment*, Wu Zhuhua (吴珠华) *et al.* (translators). Beijing Economic College Press.

Song Shiyun (宋士云) (2007). "An empirical analysis of China's residents' income from 1992 to 2001", *Researches In Chinese Economic History* (1).

The State Council Research Group (2006). *Report of Chinese Migrant Worker Survey*. China Yanshi Press.

Su Xiaoli (苏晓离) (1996). "On values in the economic distribution", *Philosophy Study* (8).

Sun Liping (孙立平) (2002). "New trends of the evolution of China's social structure since the mid-1990s", *Economic Management Digest* (23).

Sun Liping (2003). "Characteristics of the gap between the poor and rich", *Theory and Practice* (5).

Sun Liping (2008). "Social transformation: New subjects for the sociology of development", *Open Era* (2).

The CCCPC Party Literature Research Office (2004). *Yearbook of Deng Xiaoping* (2), Beijing: Central Literature Press.

Tan Zhiling (谭芝灵) (2006). "Discussion on the essence and characteristics of the polarization between the rich and poor and the polarization in China", *Productivity Research* (1).

Wan Guanghua (万广华) (2006). *Economic Development and Income Inequality: Methods and Evidence.*

Wan Guanghua (2008), "Inequality measurement and decomposition: A survey", *Economy (Quarterly)* 8(1), pp. 347–367.

Wang Xiaolu (王小鲁) (2006). "Income inequality in China and its influencing factors", Research Paper No. 2006/126, World Institute for Development Economics Research, United Nations University.

Wang Jiangui (王检贵) (2000). "Two different polarization", *Economists* (2), pp. 69–73.

Wang Minghua （王明华） (2003). "The relationship between income discrepancy and polarization", *Economic Issues* (9), pp, 2–4.

Wang Xiaolu (王小鲁) and Gang Fan (樊纲) (2005). "Income inequality in China and its influential factors", *Economic Study* (10), pp. 24–36.

Wang Xiaolu (王小鲁) (2007). "The grey income and the discrepancy of income distribution in China", *Chinese Reforms* (7), pp. 9–12.

Wang Xiaotao (王晓焘) and Hu Feng (胡丰) (2008). "Urban working youth employment income change and its cause analysis", *Youth Studies*, (2), pp. 18–21.26.

Wellman, Barry (1981). "Applying network analysis to the study of support." *In Social Network and Social Support*, B. H. Gottlieb (eds). Beverly Hills.: Sage.

Weng Dingjun (翁定军) (1999). "Analysis of social psychology to the sense of equity", *Journal of Shanghai University (Social Science Edition)* (2), pp. 49–53.

Xiong Ruimei (熊瑞梅) and Huang Yizhi (黄毅志) (1992). " Social resources and petty bourgeoisie", *Taiwanese Journal of Sociology* (16) pp. 107–138.

Xu Xianxiang (徐现祥) and Wang Haigang (王海港) (2008). "Dynamics of factor payment: evidence from China", *Economic Study* (2), pp. 106–118.

Yang Shengming (杨圣明) (2005). "On polarization in income distribution", *Consumption Economy* (6), pp. 8–14.

Zhang Guang (张光) and Liu Weiwei (刘伟伟) (2008). "Focus on the Program or Results? — An Empirical Study of College Students' sense of fairness", *Youth Studies*, (11) pp. 33–40.

Zheng Honge (郑红娥) (2006), "The evolution of consumer attitudes of youth from the media changes", *China Youth Study*, (1), pp. 16–18.

Zhang Baoping (张保平) (2007). "Manage polarization and promote harmonious development", *Market Forum* (5), pp.1–3.

Zhang Honghai (章洪海) and Gou Juanjuan (苟娟娟) (2005). "Discussion about polarization in China", *Economic Issues* (6), pp. 28–30.

Zhang Kui (张奎) and Wang Zuxiang (王祖祥) (2009), "Measurement and control of income inequality and polarization: Case of Shanghai urban residents", *Statistics study* (8), pp. 77–80

Zhang Taoxin (张陶新) (2009), "Positive analysis about the evolution of the polarity between urban and rural areas of China since the city reform", *Journal of Hunan University of Technology* (Social Science Edition) 14 (2), pp. 23–27.

Zhang Wenhong and Ruan Danqing (1999). "Social support network of urban and rural residents", *Sociological Studies* (3).

Zhao Yandong (赵延东) (2007) . "Social networks and health of urban and rural residents", *The 3rd Conference of Social Networks and Relational Management*.

Zhou Xincheng (周新城) (2006). "How to understand polarization", *Journal of Beijing Jiaotong University* (Social Sciences Edition) (4), pp. 60–64.

Zhou Xueguang (周雪光) and Hou Liren (侯立仁) (2003). The children of the Culture Revolution — Contemporary China and the life course. In the CASS Institute of Sociology Research (ed.), *Chinese Sociology (Vol. 2)*. Shanghai: Shanghai People's Publishing House.

Index